CONTENTS

The dates are those of composition, as given by Hoboken in his thematic catalogue.

JOSEPH HAYDN
Complete Piano Sonatas

IN TWO VOLUMES

VOLUME I
(Hoboken Nos. 1–29)

DOVER PUBLICATIONS, INC.
NEW YORK

Published in Canada by General Publishing Company, Ltd., 30 Lesmill Road, Don Mills, Toronto, Ontario.

Published in the United Kingdom by Constable and Company, Ltd.

This Dover edition in two volumes, first published in 1984, contains all the music from the three volumes comprising *Serie 14: Klavierwerke* [1918] of the complete-works edition *Joseph Haydns Werke. Erste kritisch durchgesehene Gesamtausgabe*, published by Breitkopf & Härtel, Leipzig, 1907 ff. The table of contents and Publisher's Note have been prepared specially for the present edition; see the Publisher's Note for further bibliographical information.

Manufactured in the United States of America
Dover Publications, Inc., 31 East 2nd Street, Mineola, N.Y. 11501

Library of Congress Cataloging in Publication Data

Haydn, Joseph, 1732–1809.
 [Sonatas, piano]
 Complete piano sonatas.

 Reprint. Originally published: Leipzig : Breitkopf & Härtel, 1918 (Joseph Haydns Werke. Erste kritisch durchgesehene Gesamtausgabe, Serie 14: Klavierwerke / edited by Karl Päsler).
 Contents: v. 1. Hoboken nos. 1-29—v. 2. Hoboken nos. 30-52.
 1. Sonatas (Piano)   I. Päsler, Karl.
M23.H41P33   1984   84-759555
ISBN 0-486-24726-0 (v. 1)
ISBN 0-486-24727-9 (v. 2)

PUBLISHER'S NOTE

The musical text of the 52 sonatas included in this two-volume Dover edition is reprinted, without abridgment or change of sequence, from the three volumes comprising *Serie 14: Klavier-werke*, n.d. [actually 1918; edited by Karl Päsler], of the Breitkopf & Härtel (Leipzig) Haydn complete-works edition inaugurated in 1907 under the general editorship of Eusebius Mandyczewski.[1]

Päsler's edition of the piano sonatas was consistently followed, with regard both to pieces included and to their sequence, by the eminent scholar Anthony van Hoboken in the section ("Gruppe XVI") devoted to the sonatas in his authoritative thematic catalogue of Haydn's works.[2] Thus, the sonata numbers used here are also the "Hoboken numbers" (XVI:1, XVI:2, etc.) of the sonatas, numbers that are more useful for reference than the misleading opus numbers sometimes associated with the pieces. The dates of composition of the sonatas supplied in the present table of contents are those given by Hoboken, not those given by Päsler.

Inasmuch as these two Dover volumes are intended primarily as a convenient and reliable playing edition, certain other types of background information have been intentionally omitted. The (German-language) editorial commentary in the Päsler edition does not appear here, chiefly for reasons of space. No attempt has been made even to summarize the extremely complex publication history of the sonatas, a number of which were

in fact originally published in the eighteenth century as the work of other composers and were first attributed to Haydn by Päsler in 1918; the reader interested in these matters should by all means consult Hoboken. For analogous reasons, names of original dedicatees are also omitted here. Moreover, the pieces are uniformly referred to here as sonatas, even though some were originally published with such titles as partita and divertimento.

Nevertheless, despite the intentionally unpedantic approach taken in the present edition, it is only proper to point out that not all 52 sonatas included here are universally accepted as authentic works by Haydn. To take a highly significant instance of dissent, the catalogue of Haydn's works compiled by Georg Feder for the 1980 *New Grove Dictionary of Music and Musicians*[3] considers eleven of the Hoboken/Päsler sonatas as doubtful attributions, and two of them as absolutely spurious; see the Grove article for detailed reasons and suggested reattributions (the dates of composition given in Grove for many of the sonatas also differ from Hoboken's). The 47 sonatas listed in Grove as absolutely authentic include the remaining 39 Hoboken/Päsler sonatas, seven lost works and one fragment included by Hoboken under a different category ("Gruppe XIV," *Divertimenti mit Klavier*).

Following is a three-way concordance of the sonatas making use of the 52 Hoboken "authentic" numbers, the 47 Grove "authentic" numbers and the frequently used 62 WU numbers ("Wiener Urtext," i.e. *J. Haydn: Sämtliche Klaviersonaten*, 3 vols., ed. by C. Landon, Vienna, 1964–66).

---

[1] *Joseph Haydns Werke. Erste kritisch durchgesehene Gesamtausgabe.* In the three-volume *Serie 14*, the first volume contained Sonatas 1–22; the second, 23–38; the third, 39–52.

[2] *Joseph Haydn. Thematisch-bibliographisches Werkverzeichnis zusammengestellt von Anthony van Hoboken*, B. Schott's Söhne, Mainz, 1957.

---

[3] Edited by Stanley Sadie; Macmillan Publishers Limited, London.

Concordance tables (HOBOKEN / GROVE / WU).

HOBOKEN	GROVE	WU
1	doubtful	10
2	doubtful	11
3	3	14
4	4	9
5	doubtful	8
6	1	13
7	doubtful	14
8	doubtful	19
9	doubtful	18
10	doubtful	17
11	doubtful	16
12	doubtful	12
13	doubtful	15

HOBOKEN	GROVE	WU
14	15	16
15	16	21
16	spurious	22
17	spurious	23
18	doubtful	24
19	14	25
20	17	26
21	20	27
22	21	28
23	22	29
24	23	30
25	24	31
26	25	32
27	25	33
28	26	34
29	27	35
30	28	36
31	29	37
32	30	38
33	31	39
34	32	—
35	33	—
36	34	—
37	35	—
38	36	—
39	37	—

HOBOKEN	GROVE	WU
40	40	49
41	41	50
42	42	51
43	43	52
44	44	53
45	45	54
46	46	55
47	47	56
48	48	57
49	49	58
50	50	59
51	51	60
52	52	61
12	57 (& 19)	58
16	31	59
13	29	35
18	32	34
37	35	32

GROVE	HOBOKEN	WU
1	6	13
2	14	16
3	3	14
4	4	9
(lost)	4	9
47	12	21–27
57 (& 19)		
21–27	5–11	
45	13	18
19	14	19
(fragment)	15	20
46	16	21
31	17	22
20	18	23
18	19	24
28	20	25
27	21	26
26	22	27
25	23	28

GROVE	HOBOKEN	WU
32	44	29
36	21	30
37	22	31
38	23	32
39	24	33
40	25	34
41	26	35
42	27	36
43	28	37
44	29	38
45	30	39

GROVE	HOBOKEN	WU
46	31	37
47	32	19
48	35	20
49	36	21
50	37	22
51	38	23
52	39	24
53	34	25
54		

WU	HOBOKEN	GROVE
1	8	doubtful
2	7	doubtful
3	9	doubtful
4	doubtful	4
5	11	doubtful
6	10	doubtful
7	—	doubtful
8	5	doubtful
9	4	4
10	1	doubtful
11	2	doubtful
12	12	doubtful
13	6	1
14	3	3

WU	HOBOKEN	GROVE
15	13	13
16	14	2
17	—	doubtful
18	—	doubtful
19	18	12(a)
20	19	17
21	20	—
22	21	—
23	22	2 a–h (lost)
24	23	(fragment)
25	24	15
26	25	5–11
27	26	16
28	27	13
29	28	14
30	29	45
31	30	46
32	31	19
33	32	20
34	33	38

WU	HOBOKEN	GROVE
35	43	37
36	42	19
37	41	20
38	40	21
39	39	22
40	40	23
41	41	24
42	42	25
43	43	26
44	44	27
45	45	28
46	46	29
47	47	30
48	48	31

WU	HOBOKEN	GROVE
49	36	32
50	37	33
51	38	34
52	39	12(b)
53	34	42
54	40	41
55	41	40
56	42	34
57	47	35
58	48	43
59	49	44
60	50	46
61	51	47
62	52	45

Sonata No. 1 in C Major

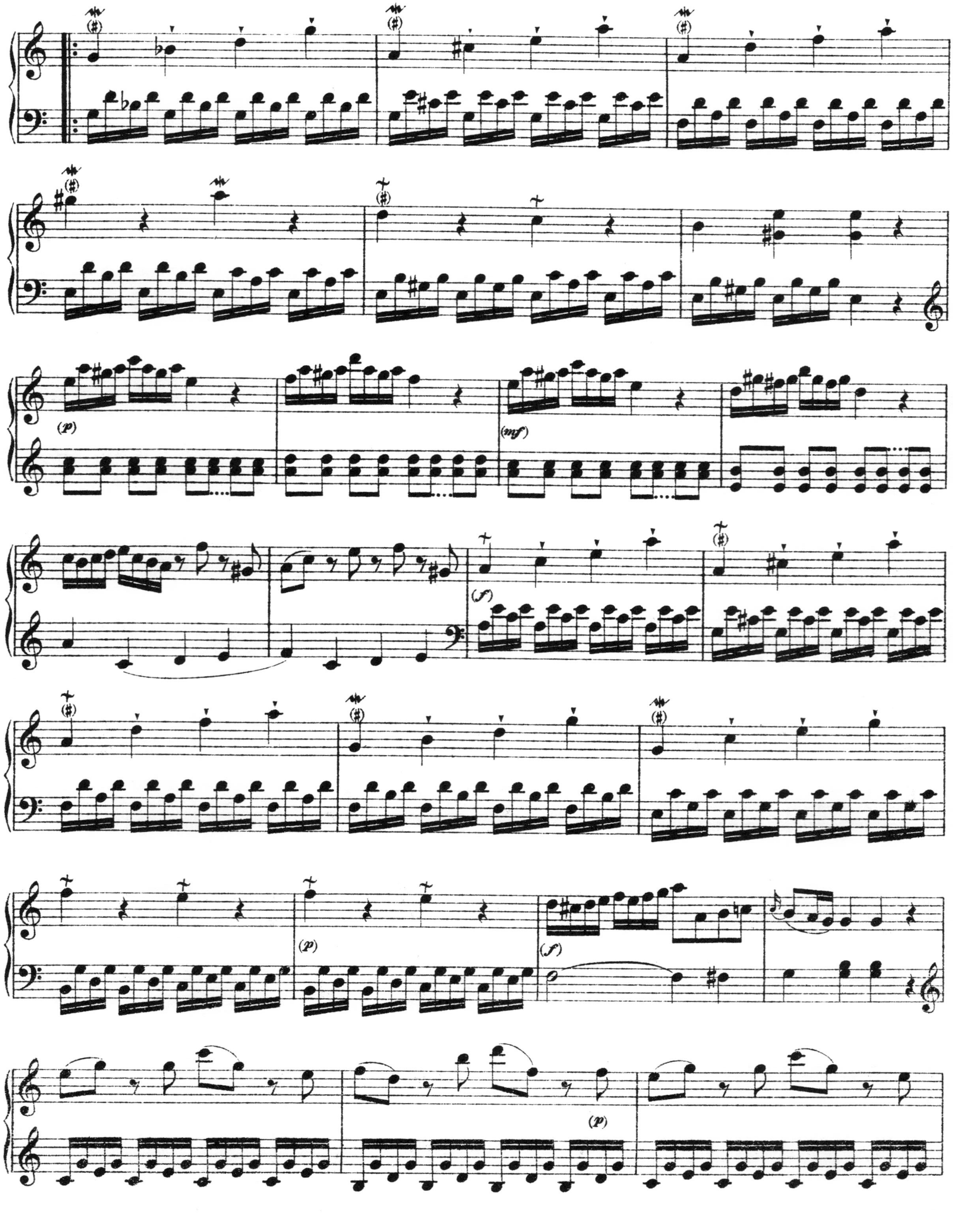
(p)
(mf)
(f)
(p)
(f)
(p)

Andante.

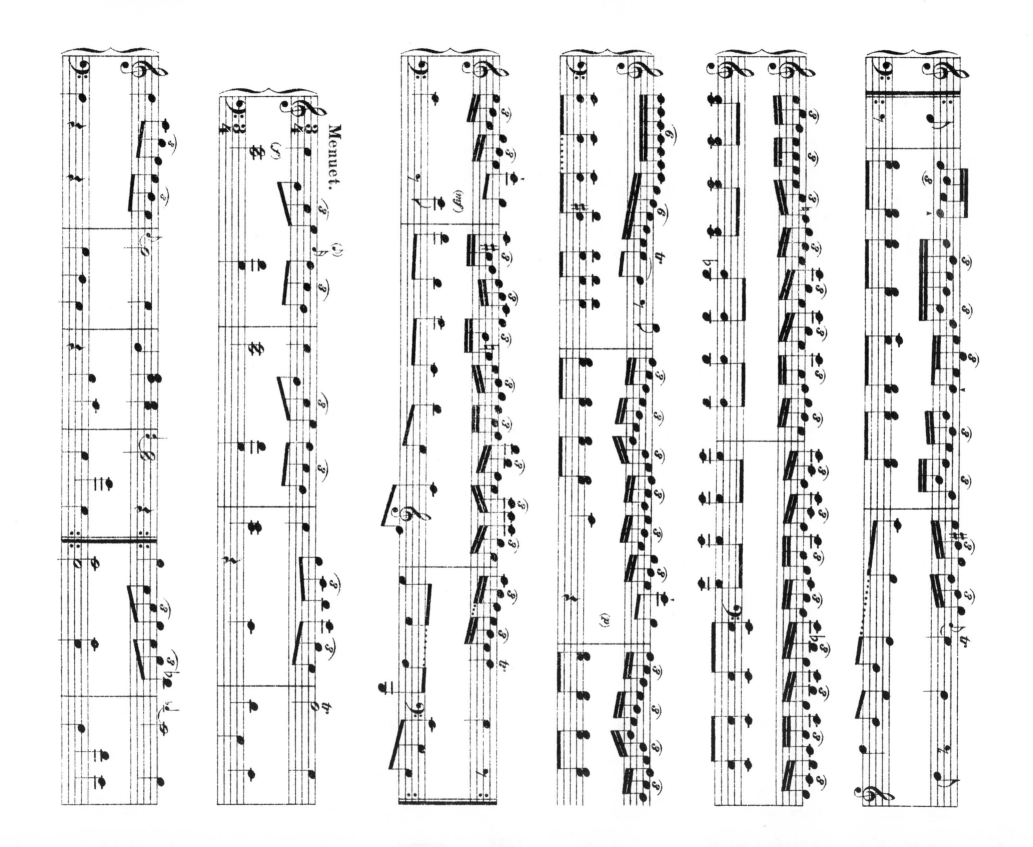

Menuet.

Sonata No. 2 in B-flat Major

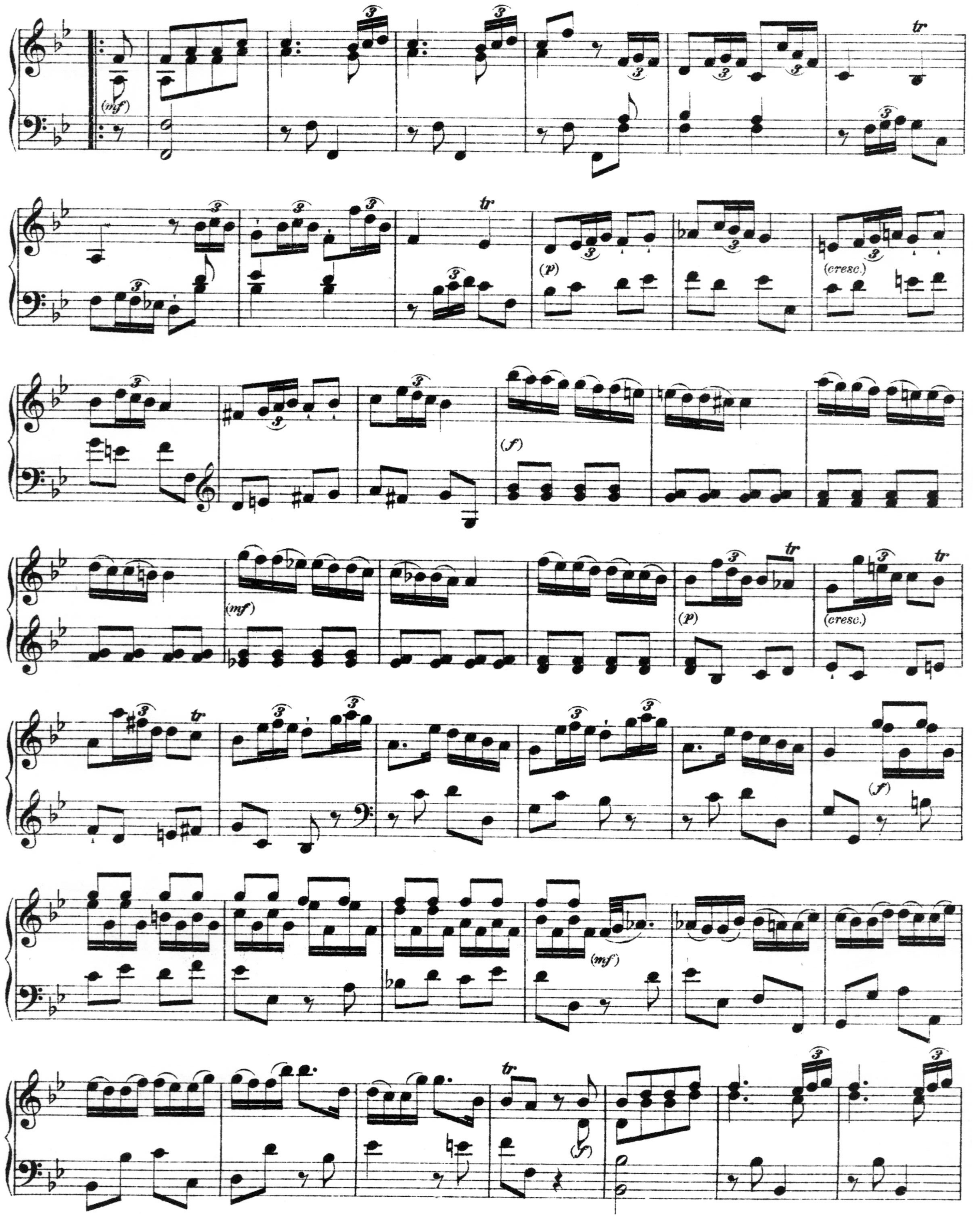
(mf)
tr
(p)
(cresc.)
(f)
(mf)
(p)
(cresc.)
tr
(f)
(mf)
tr
(f)

Largo. (Molto espressivo.)

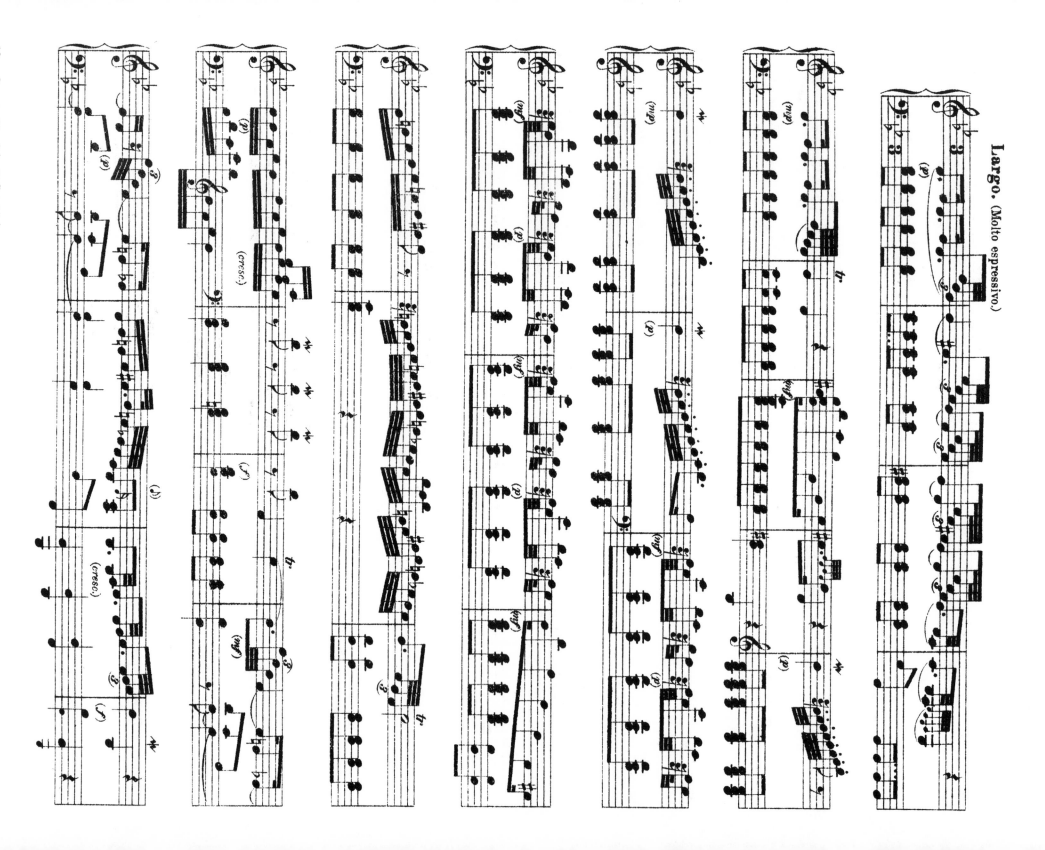

Menuet.

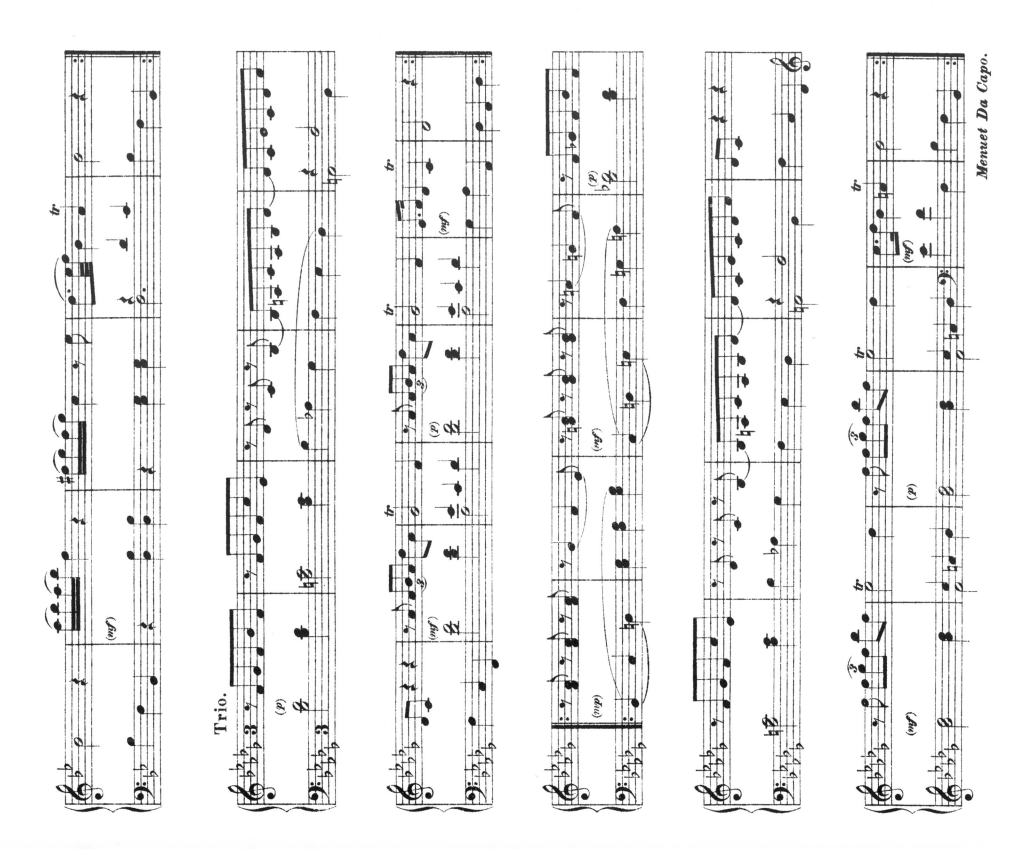

Menuet Da Capo.

Trio.

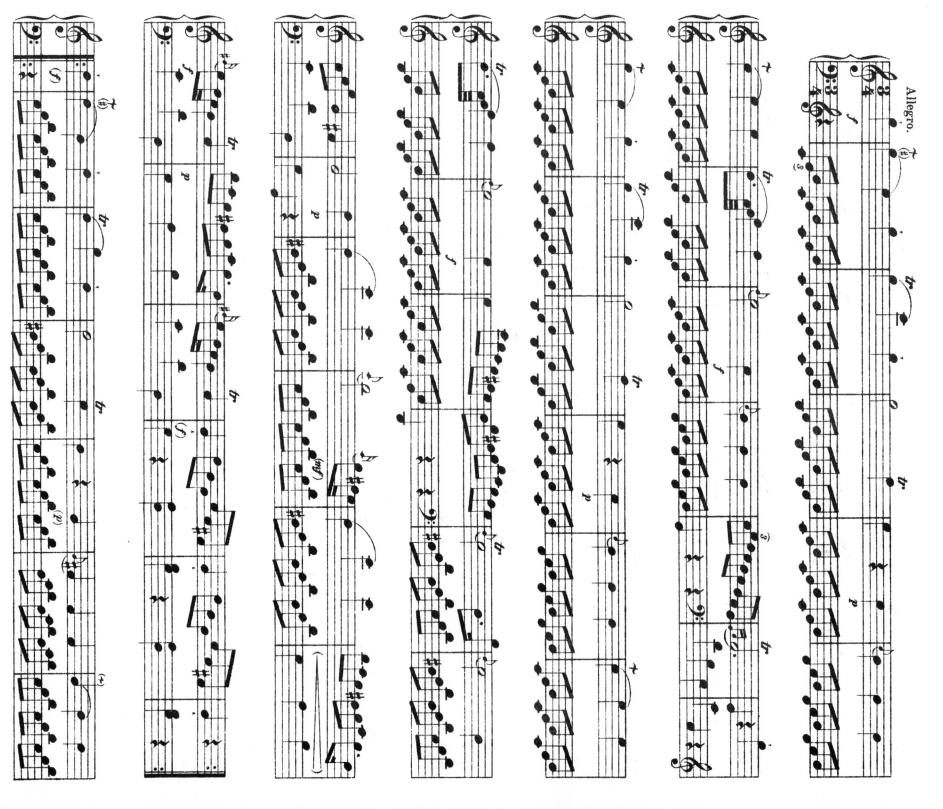

Sonata No. 3 in C Major

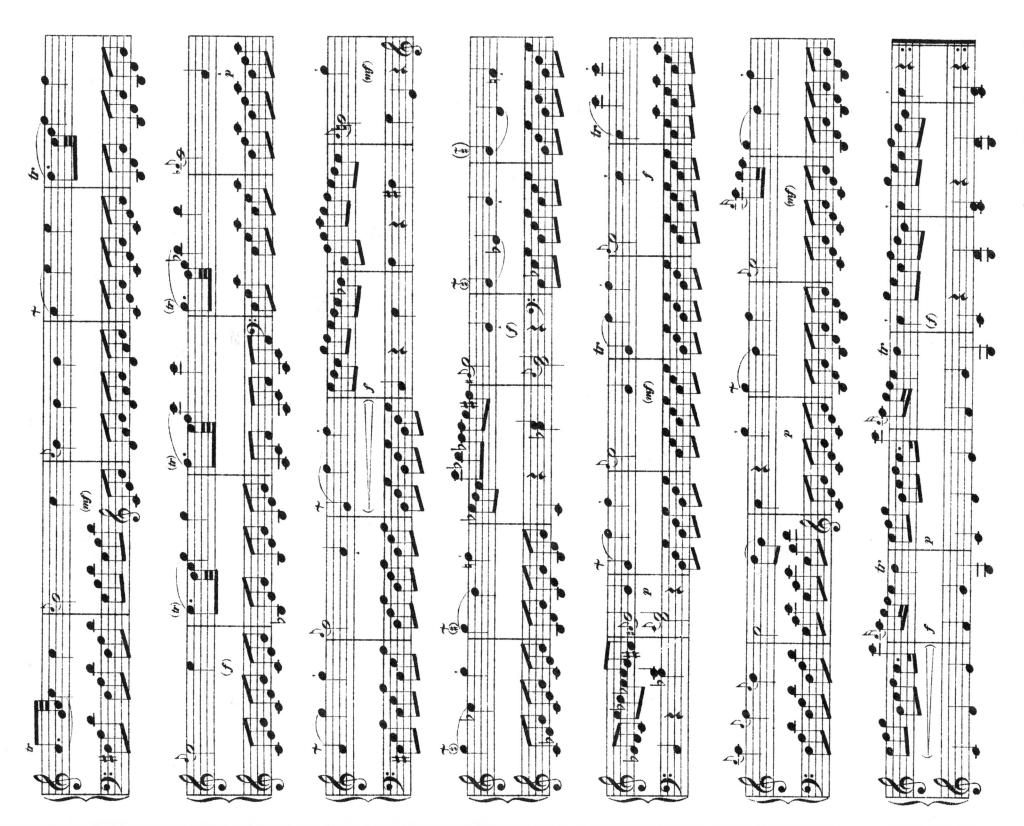

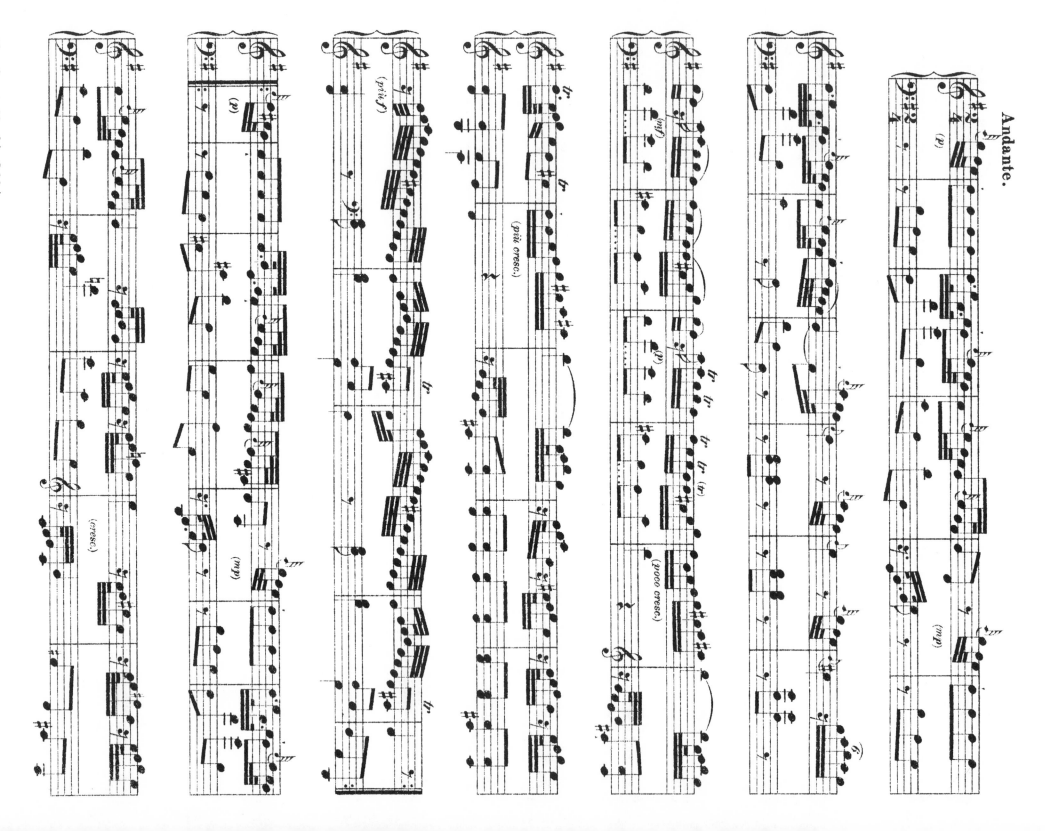

Andante.

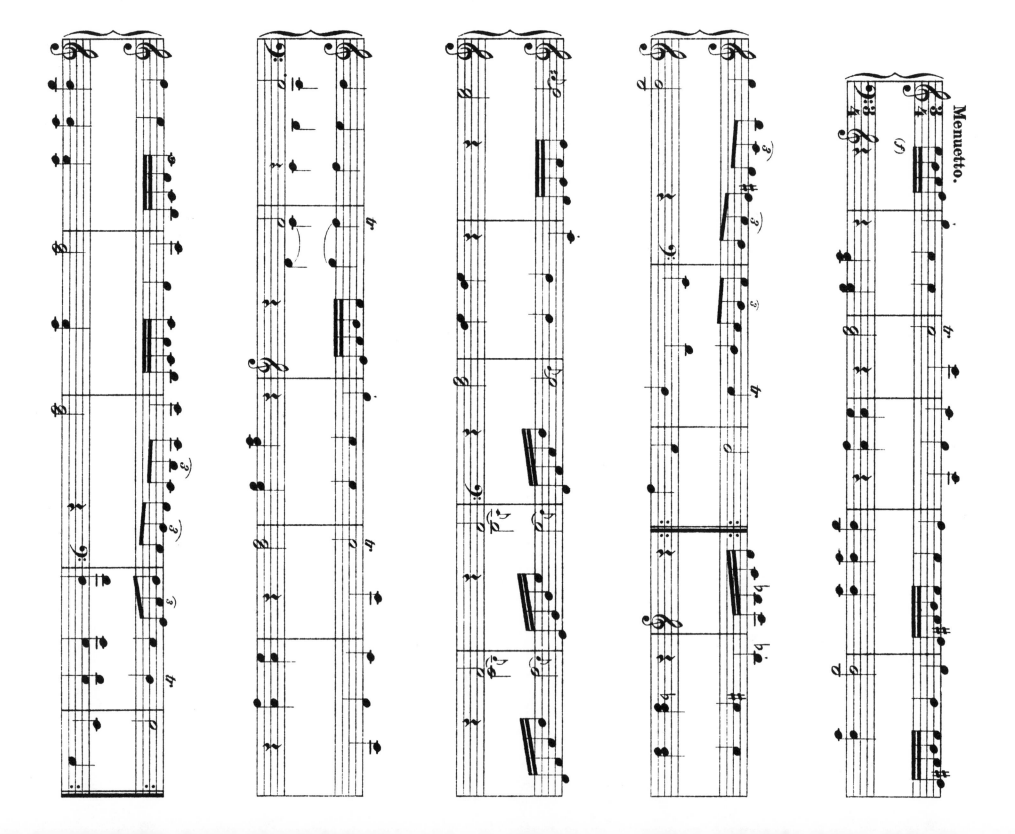

Menuetto.

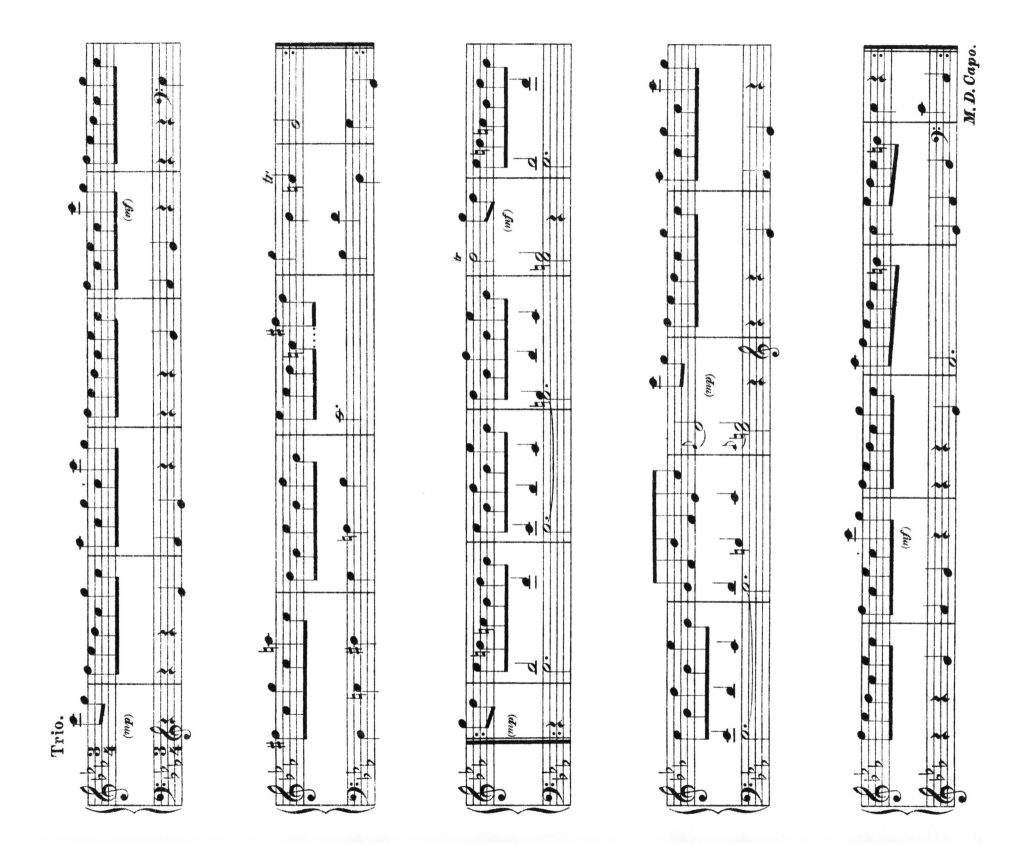

Sonata No. 4 in D Major

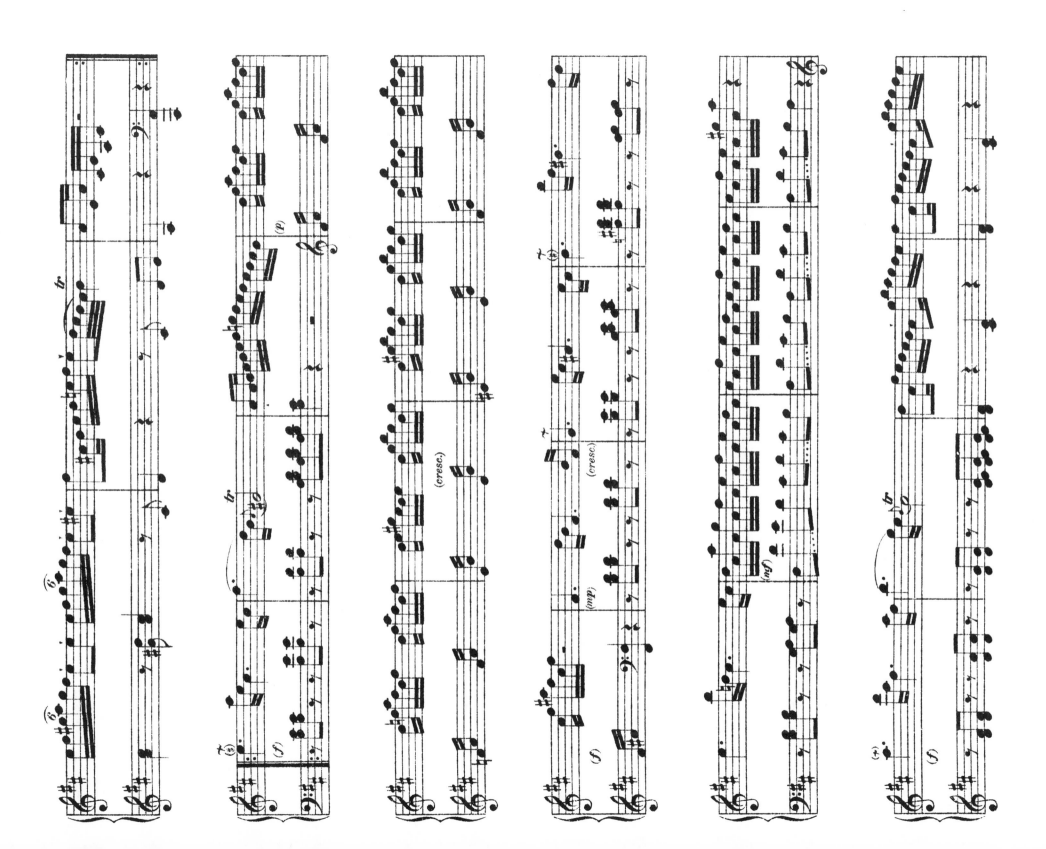

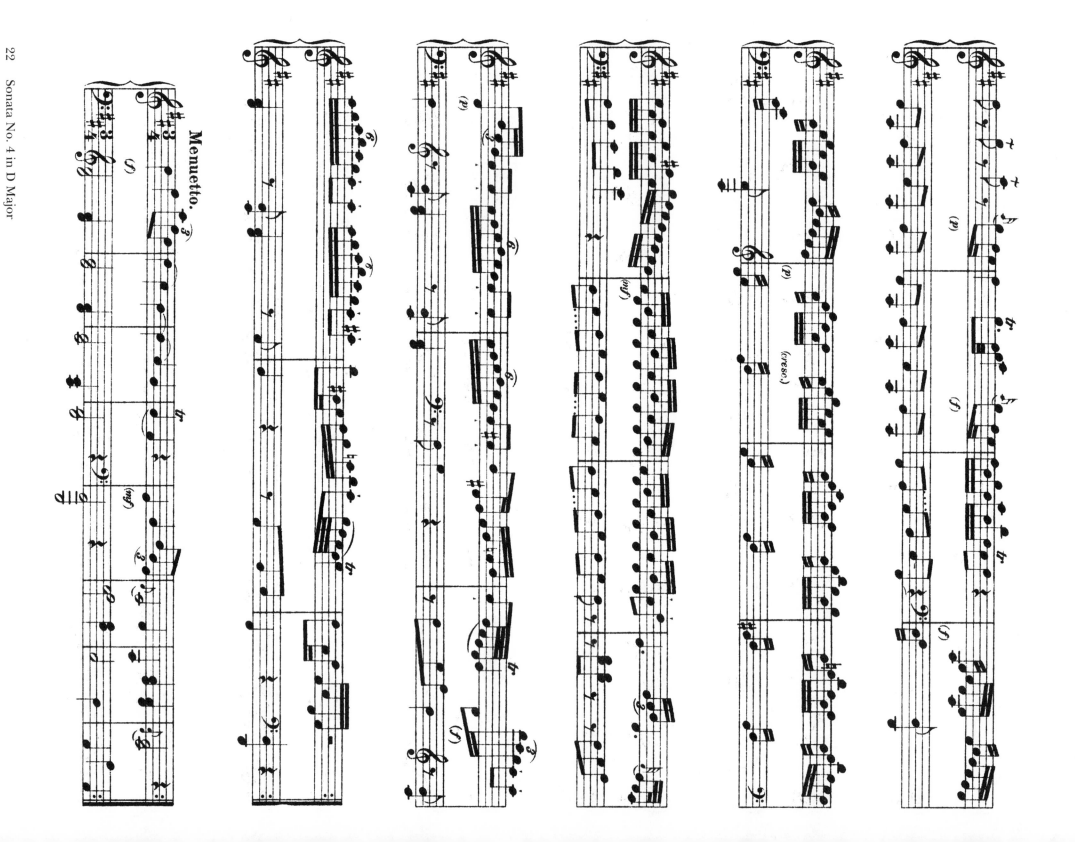

Menuetto.

Trio.

(Men. da capo)

M.D.Capo

Trio.

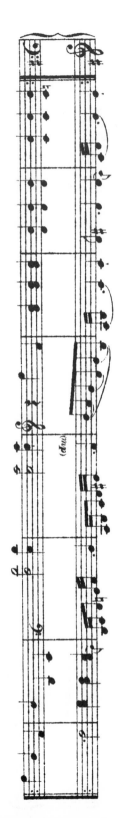

Menuet.

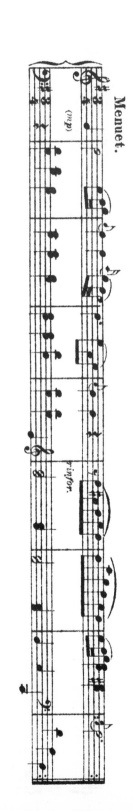

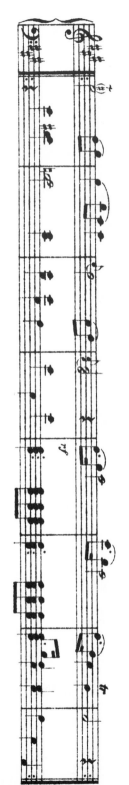

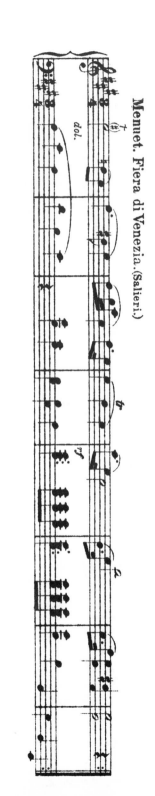

Menuet. Fiera di Venezia.(Salieri.)

Sonata No. 5 in A Major

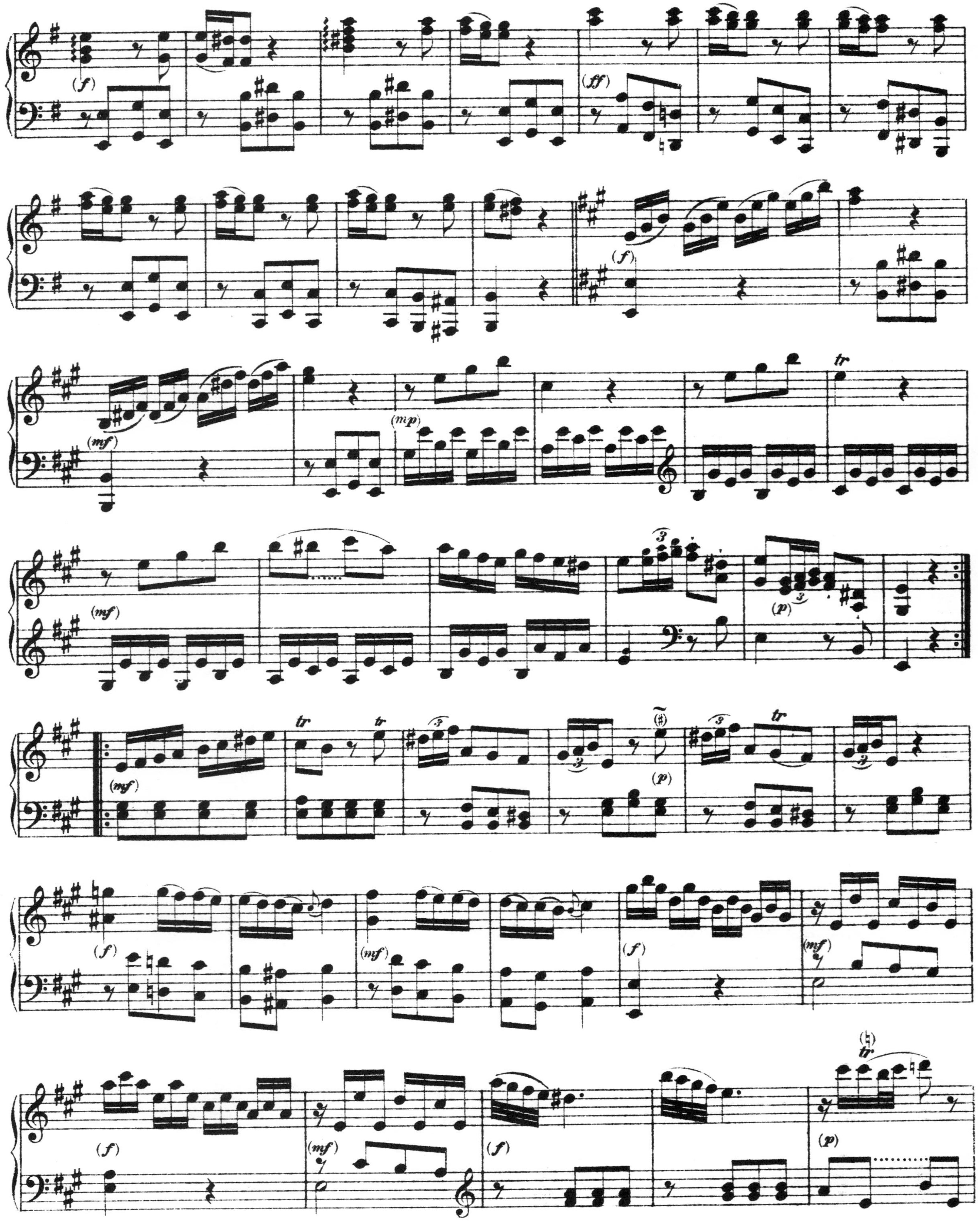
(f)
(ff)
(f)
(mf)
(mp)
tr
(mf)
3
(p)
(mf)
tr
tr
(p)
(f)
(mf)
(f)
(mf)
(f)
(mf)
(f)
(p)

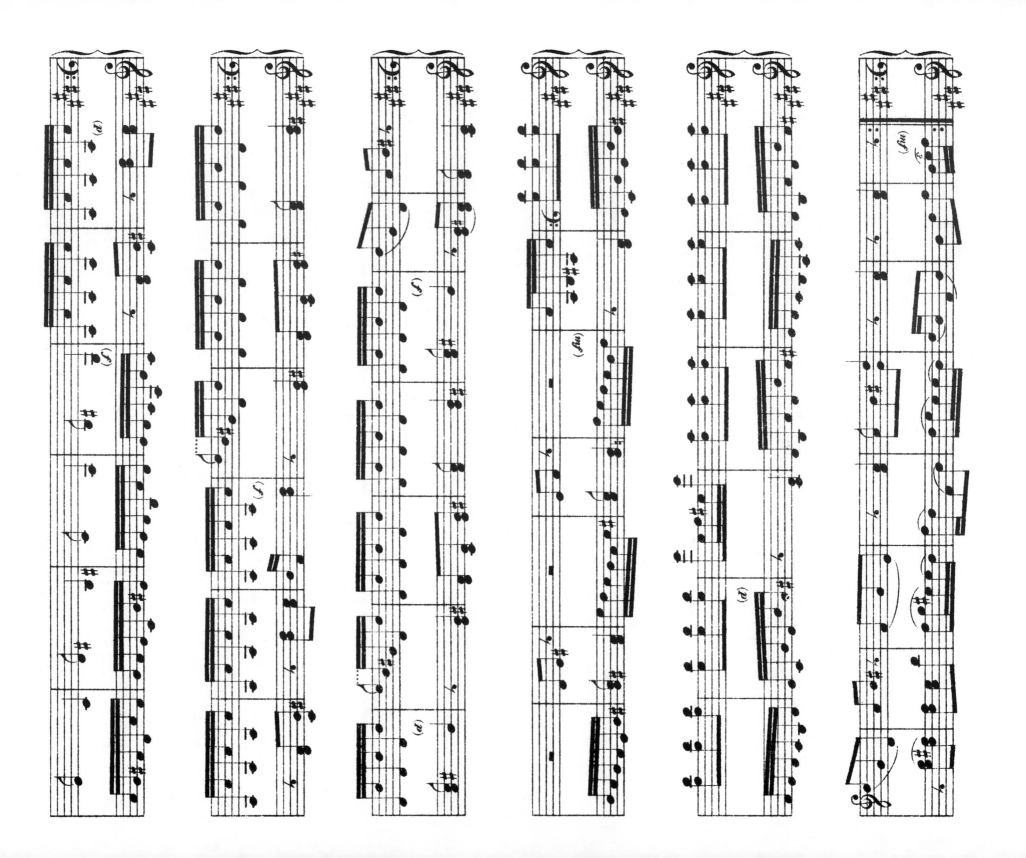

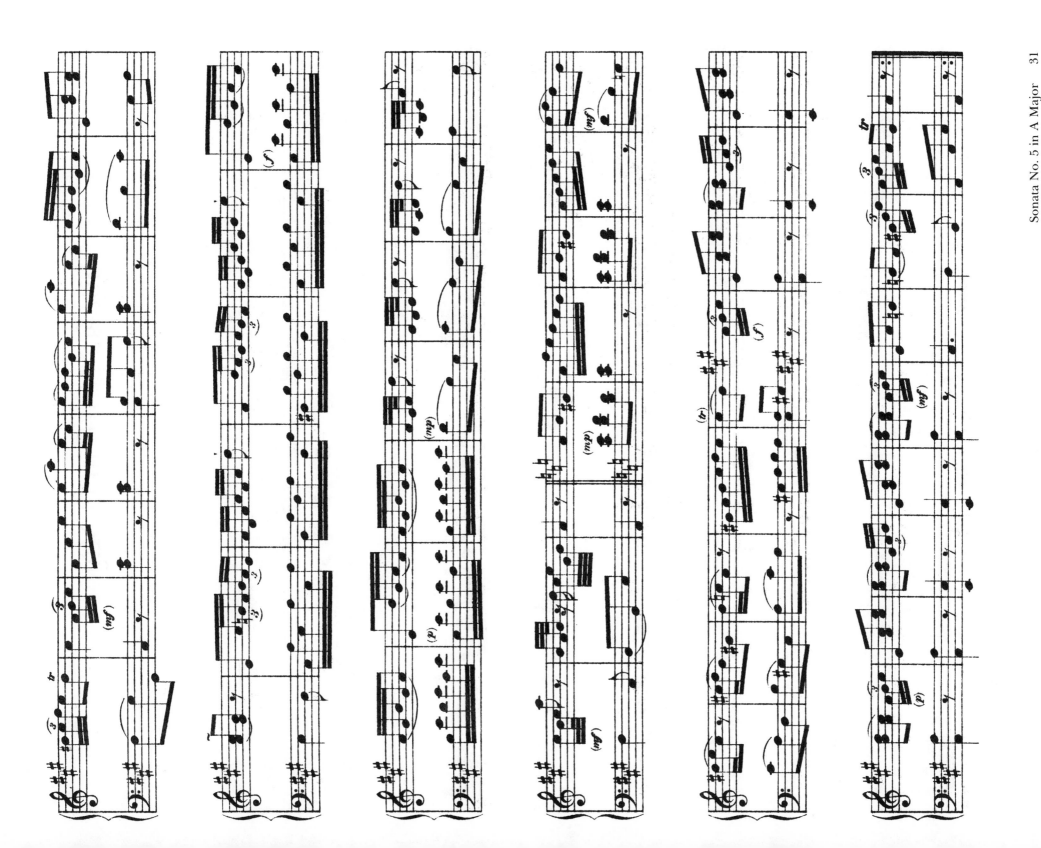

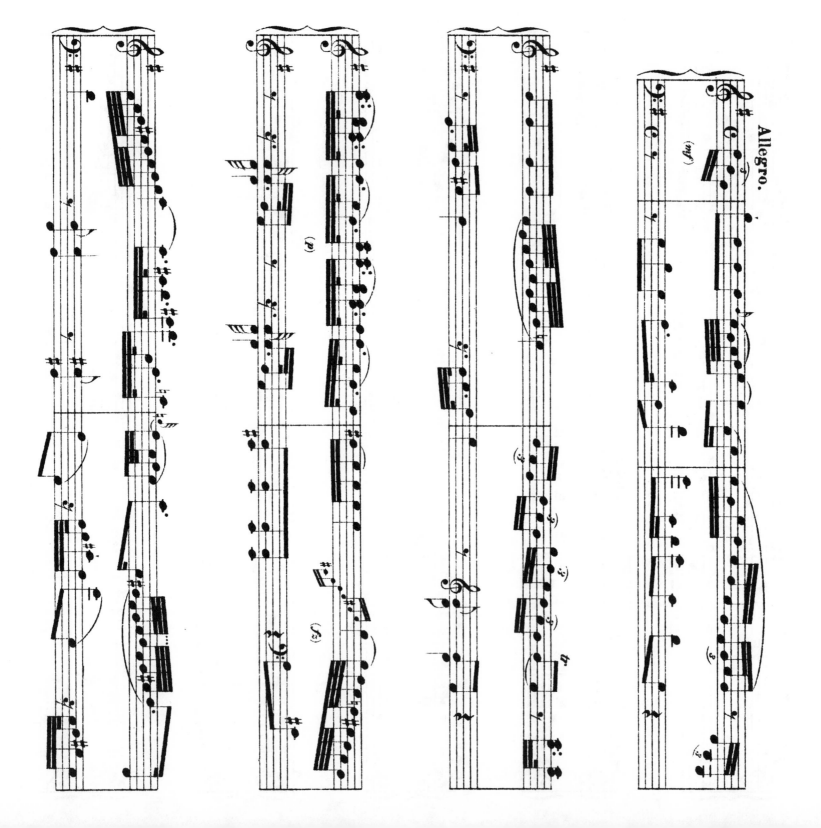

Sonata No. 6 in G Major

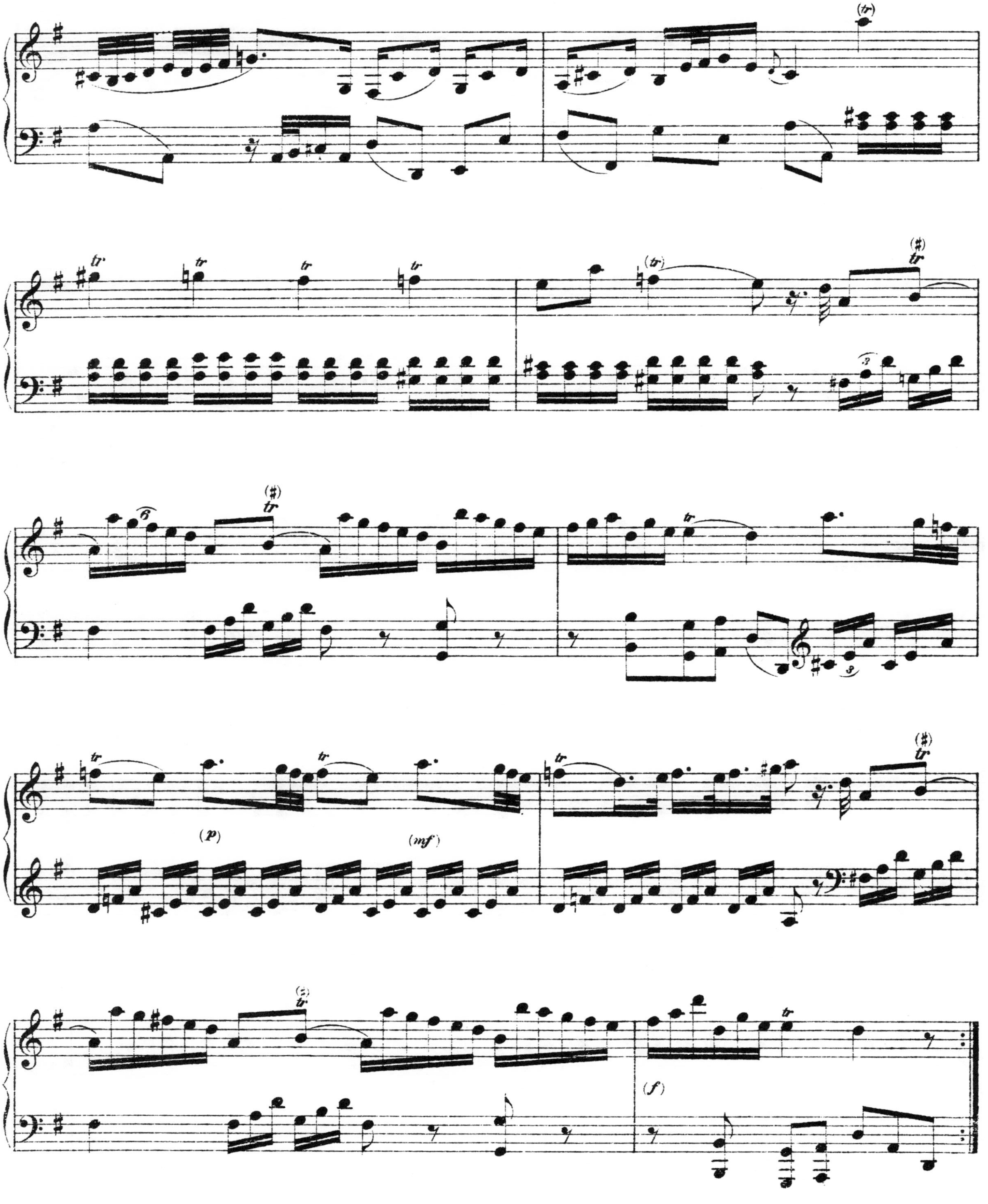
(p)
(mf)
(f)

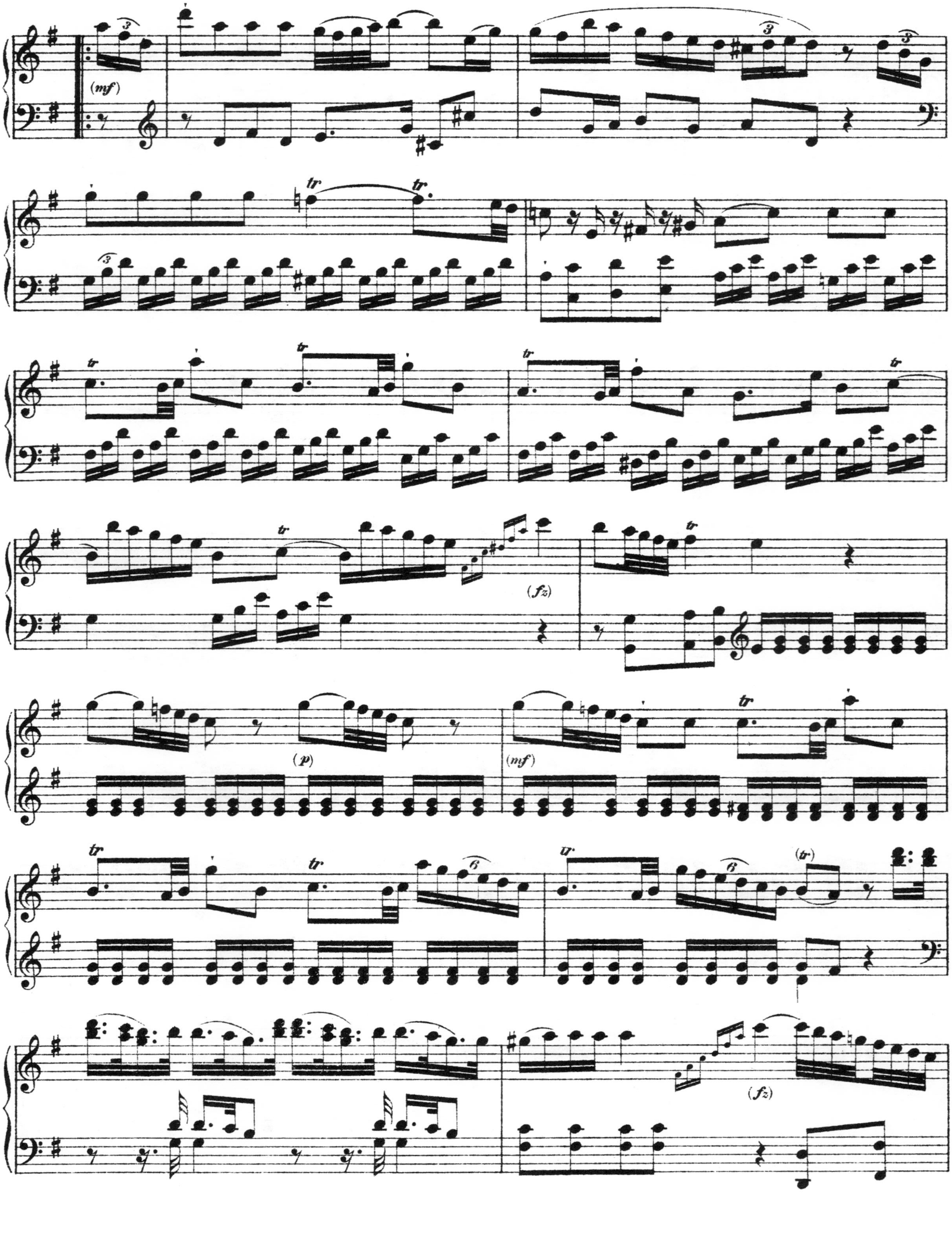
(mf)
tr
(p)
(mf)
(fz)
(tr)

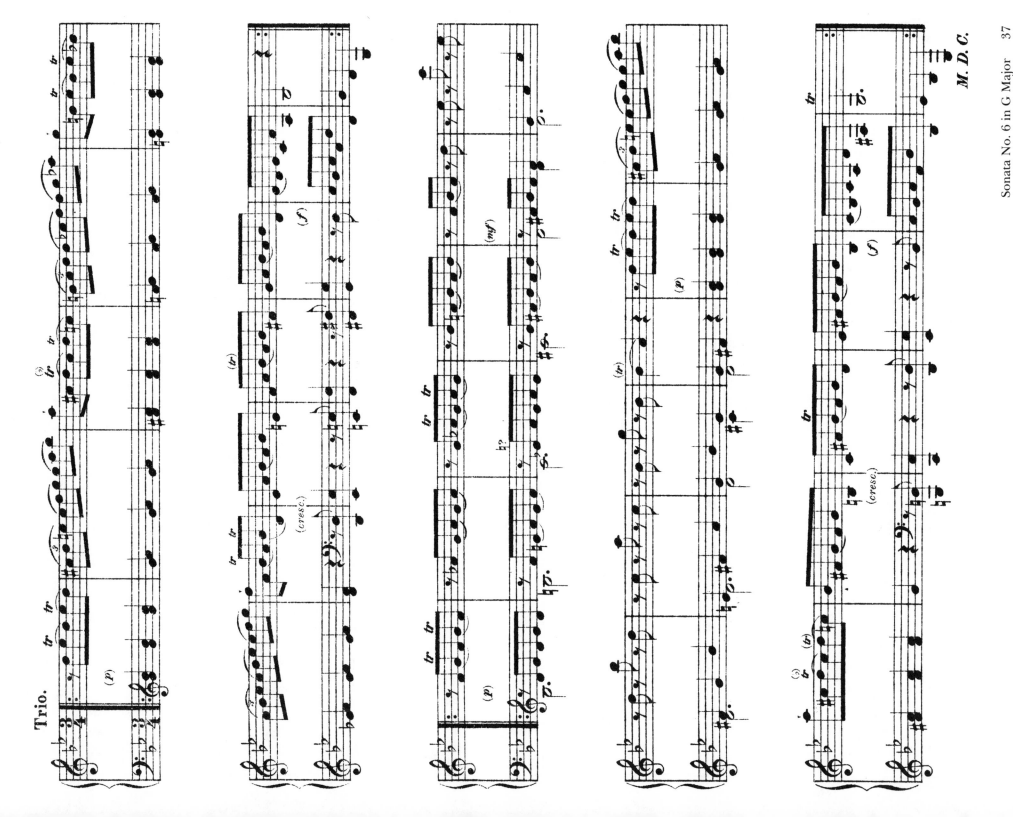

M. D. C.

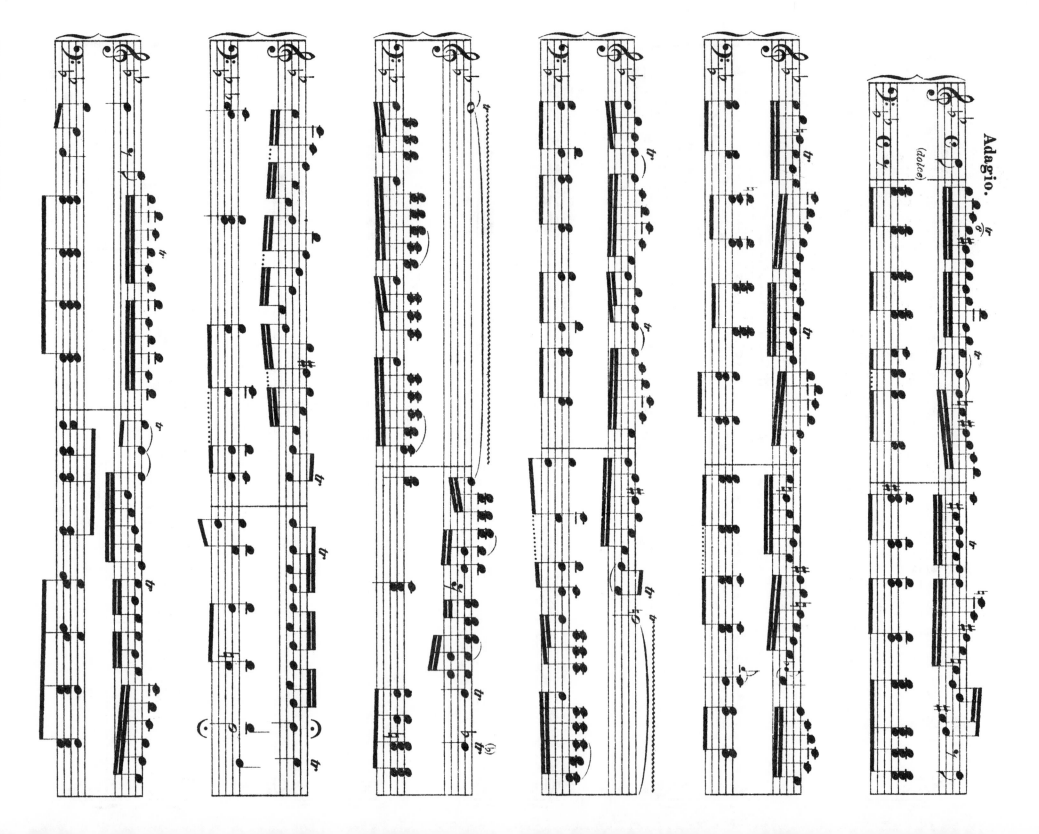

Allegro molto.

Sonata No. 7 in C Major

Allegro moderato.

Menuet.

Trio.

42

Sonata No. 8 in G Major

Allegro.

44

Sonata No. 9 in F Major

Menuet.

Trio.

Scherzo.
Allegro (non troppo).

Men. Da Capo.

Sonata No. 10 in C Major

Moderato.

Menuet.

Trio.

Menuet Da Capo.

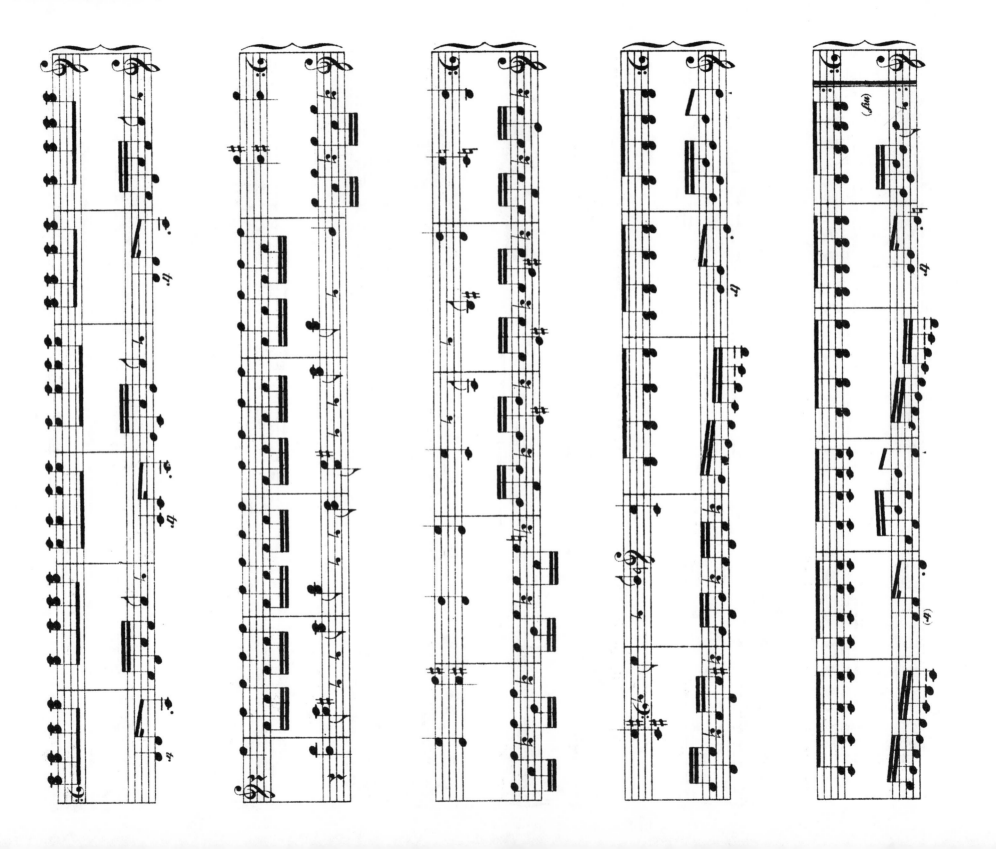

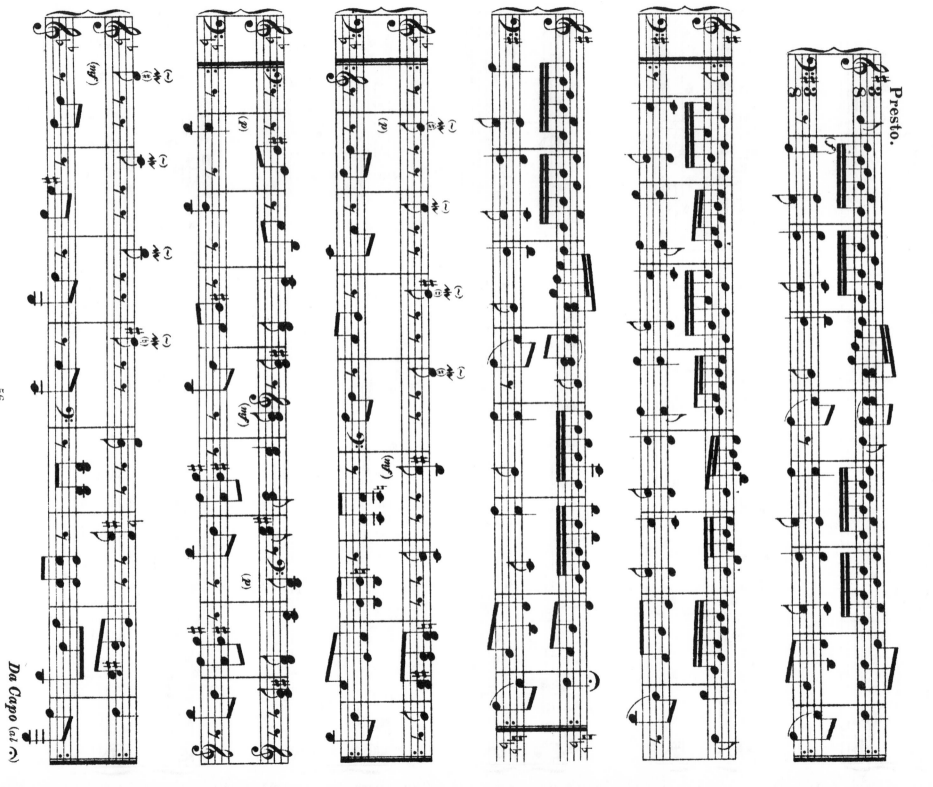

Sonata No. 11 in G Major

Presto.

Da Capo (al ↷)

Menuet.

Menuet Da Capo.

Trio.

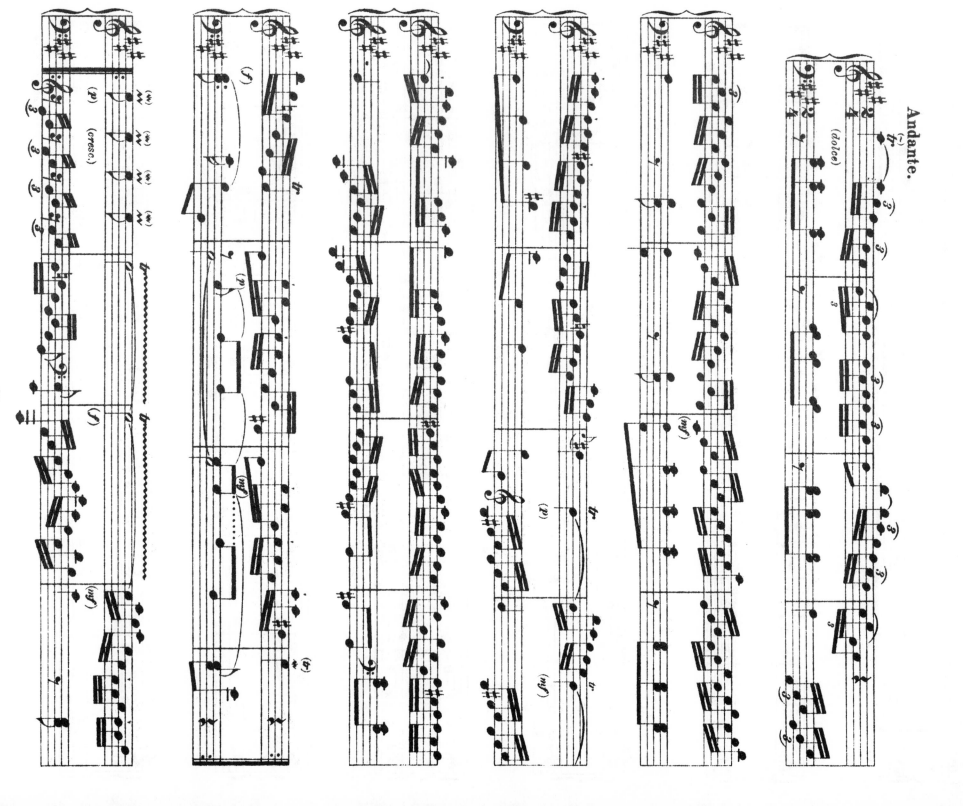

Sonata No. 12 in A Major

60

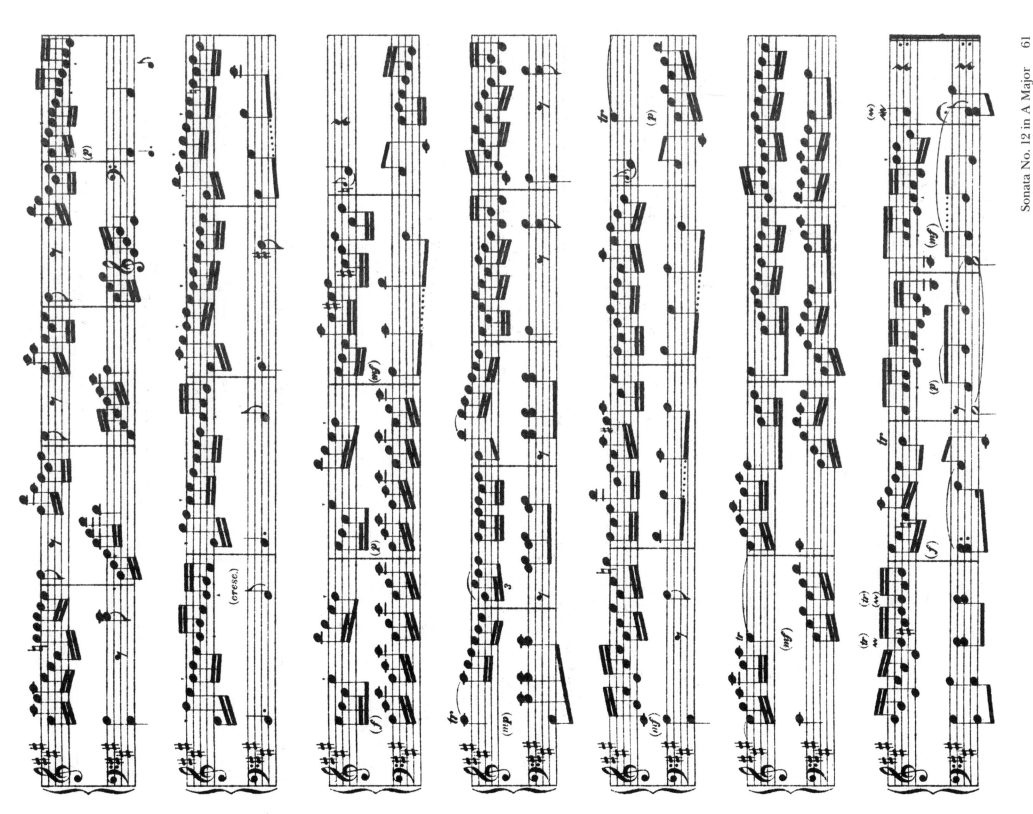

Menuetto.

Trio.
(Minore.)

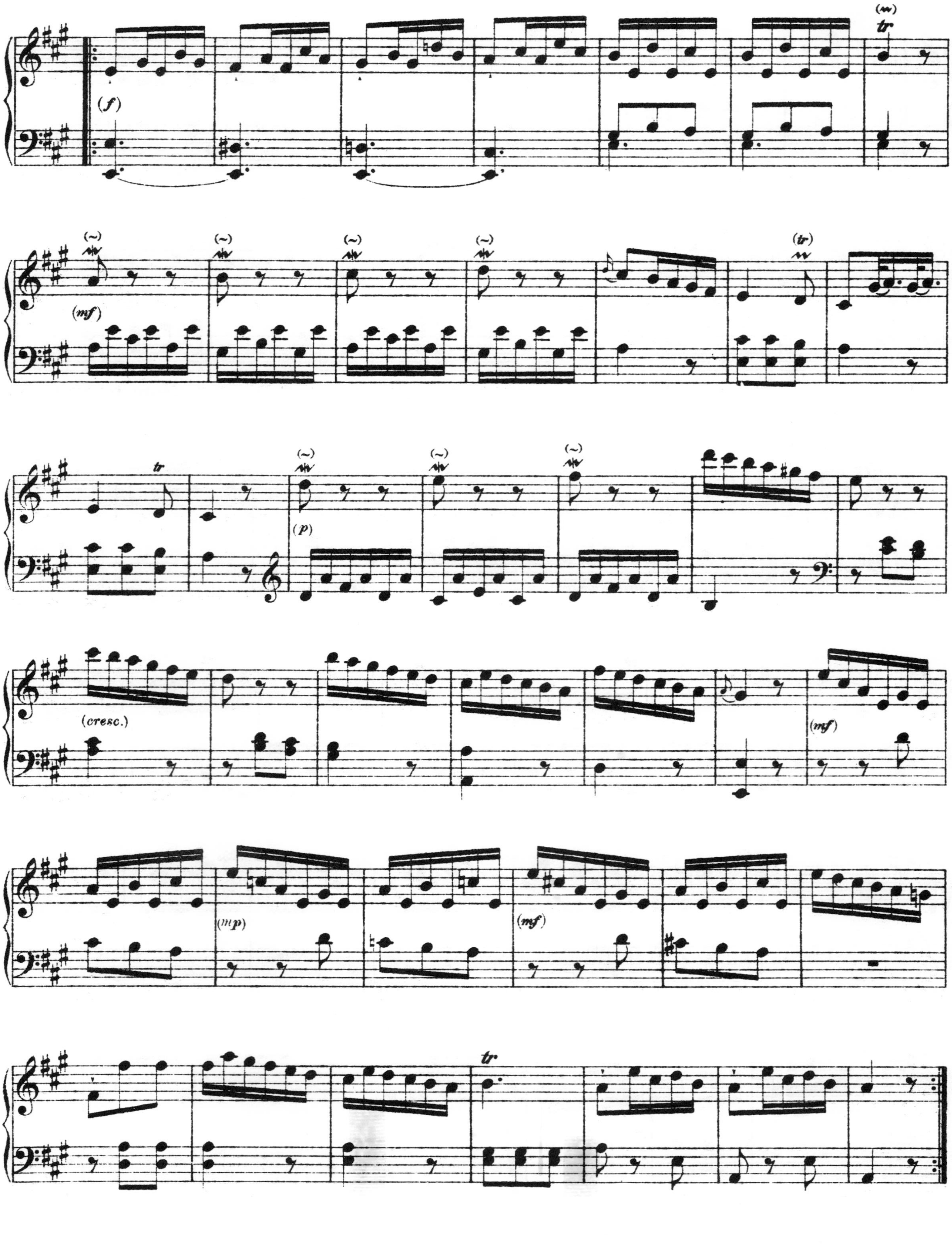
(f)
(mf)
(p)
(cresc.)
(mf)
(mp)
(mf)

Sonata No. 13 in E Major

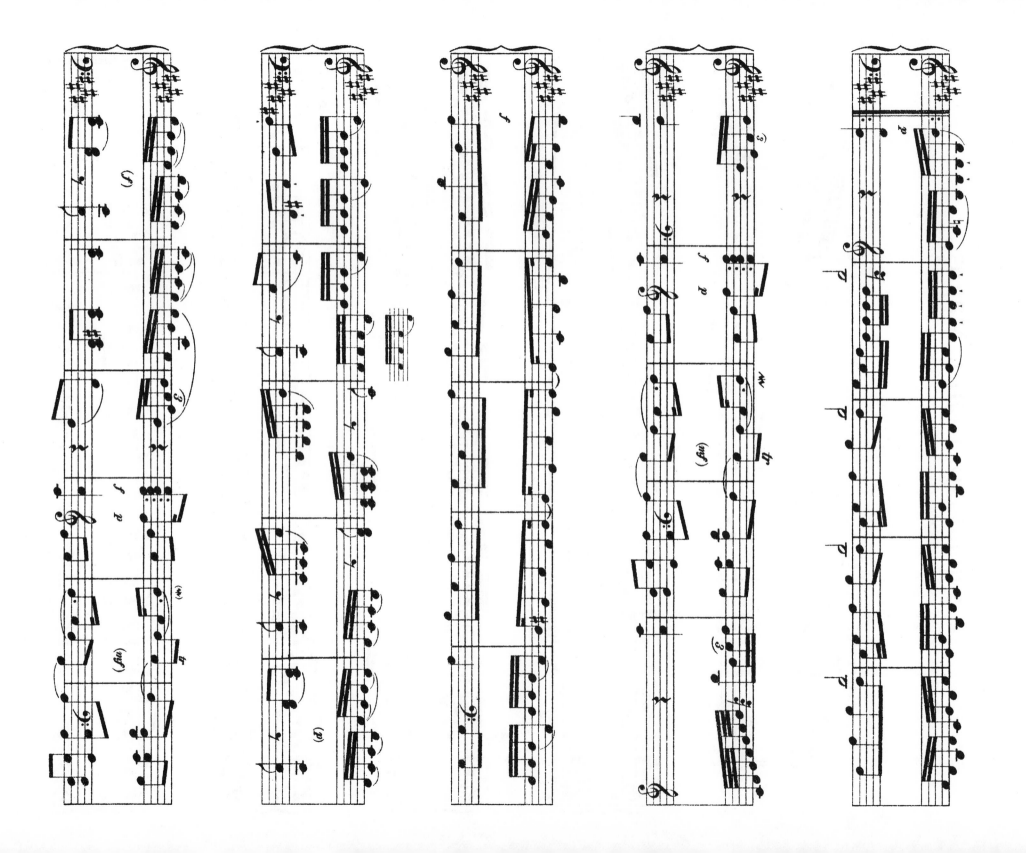

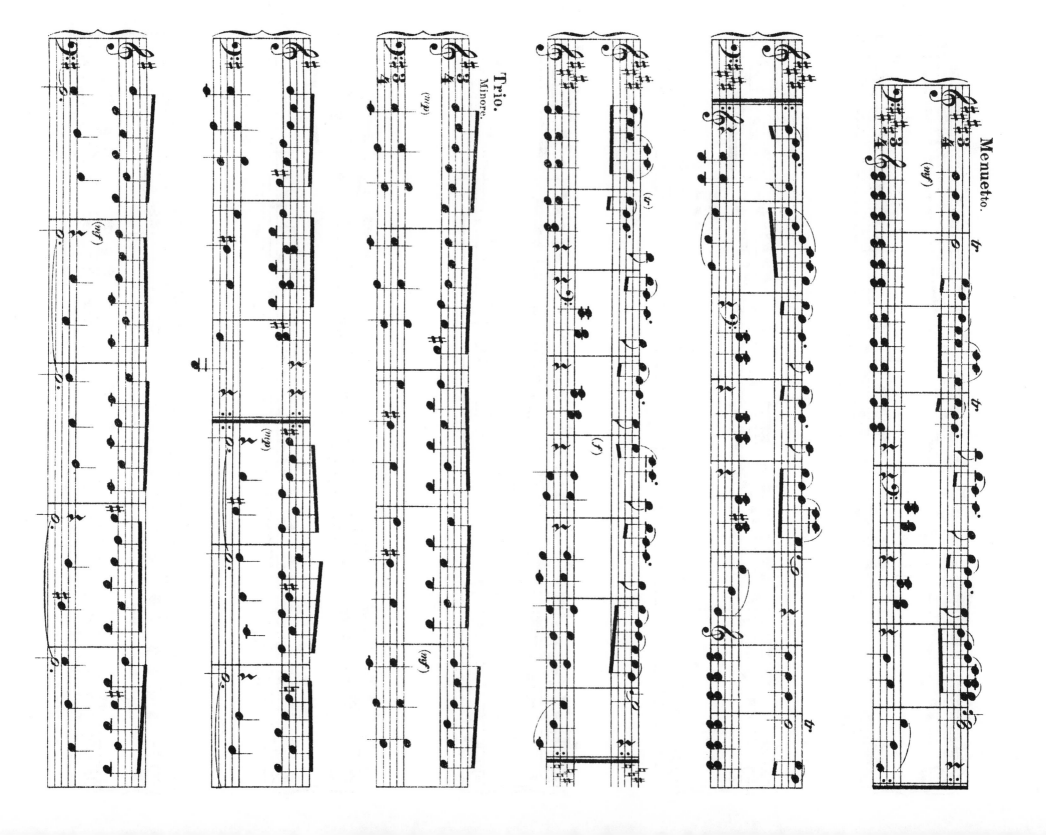

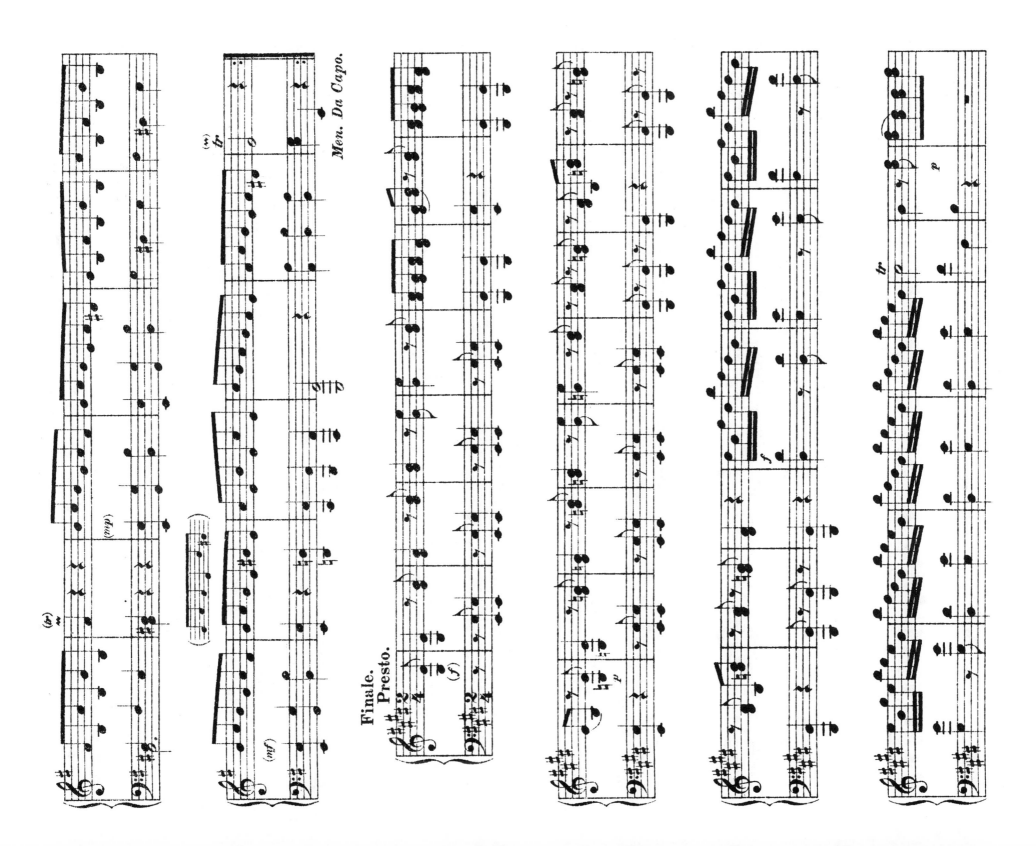

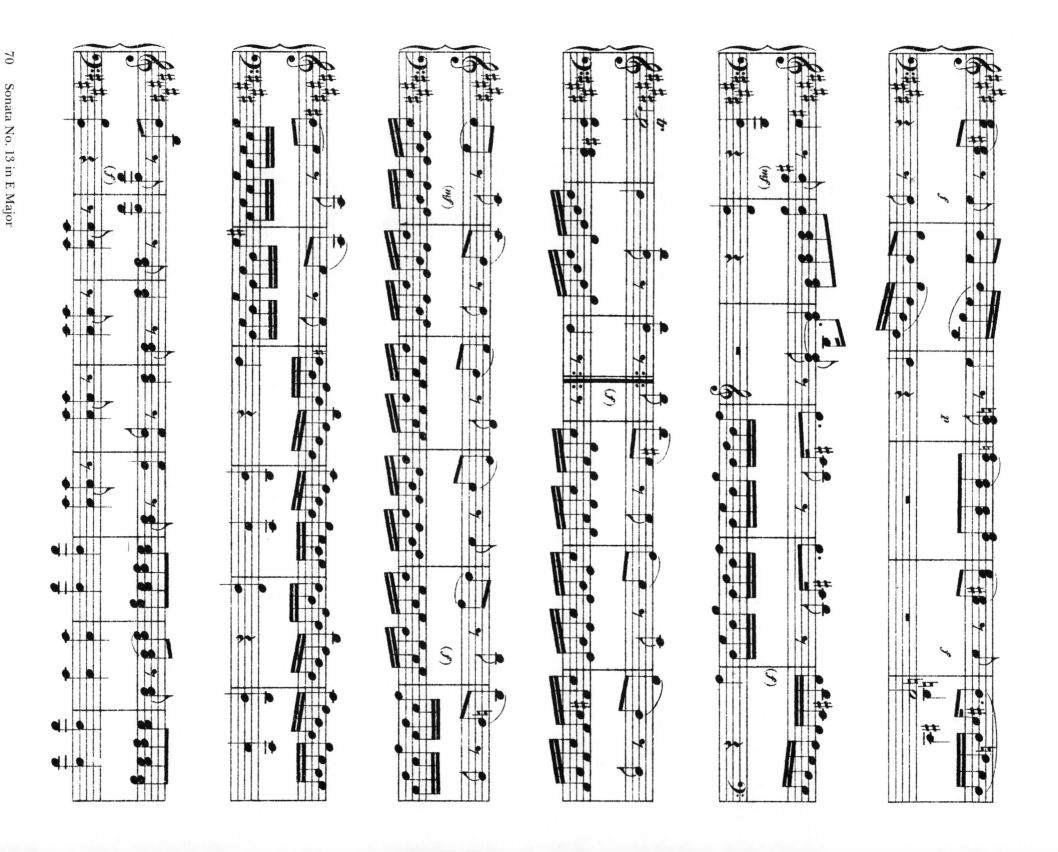

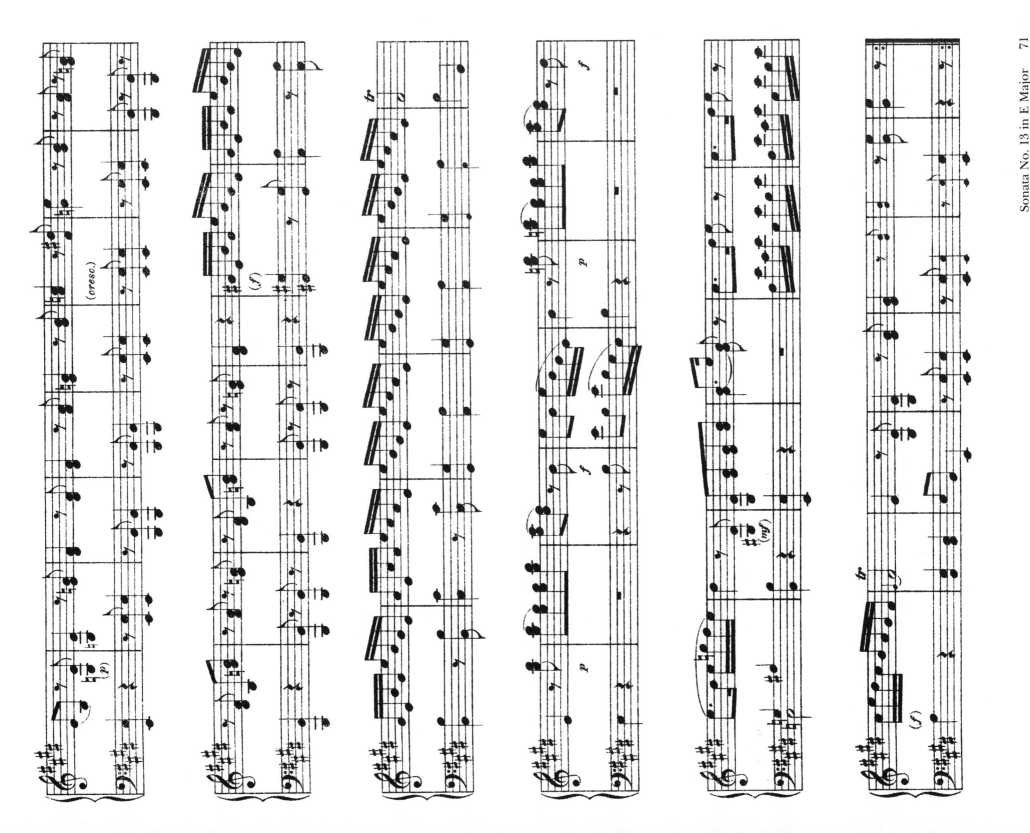

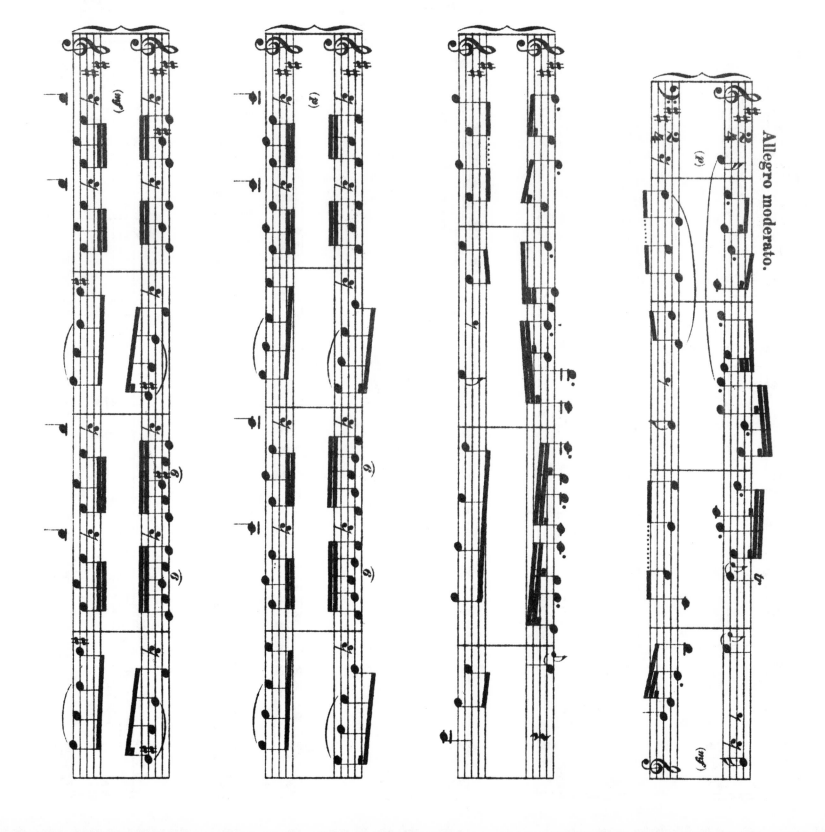

Sonata No. 14 in D Major

Allegro moderato.

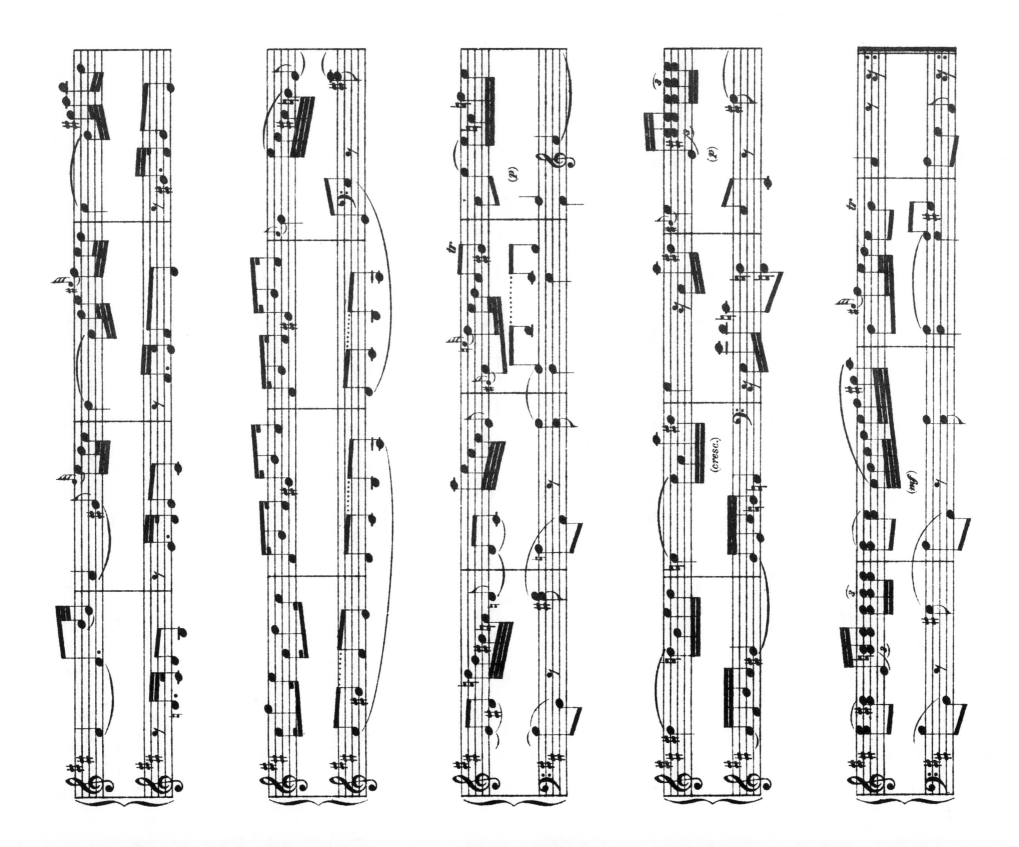

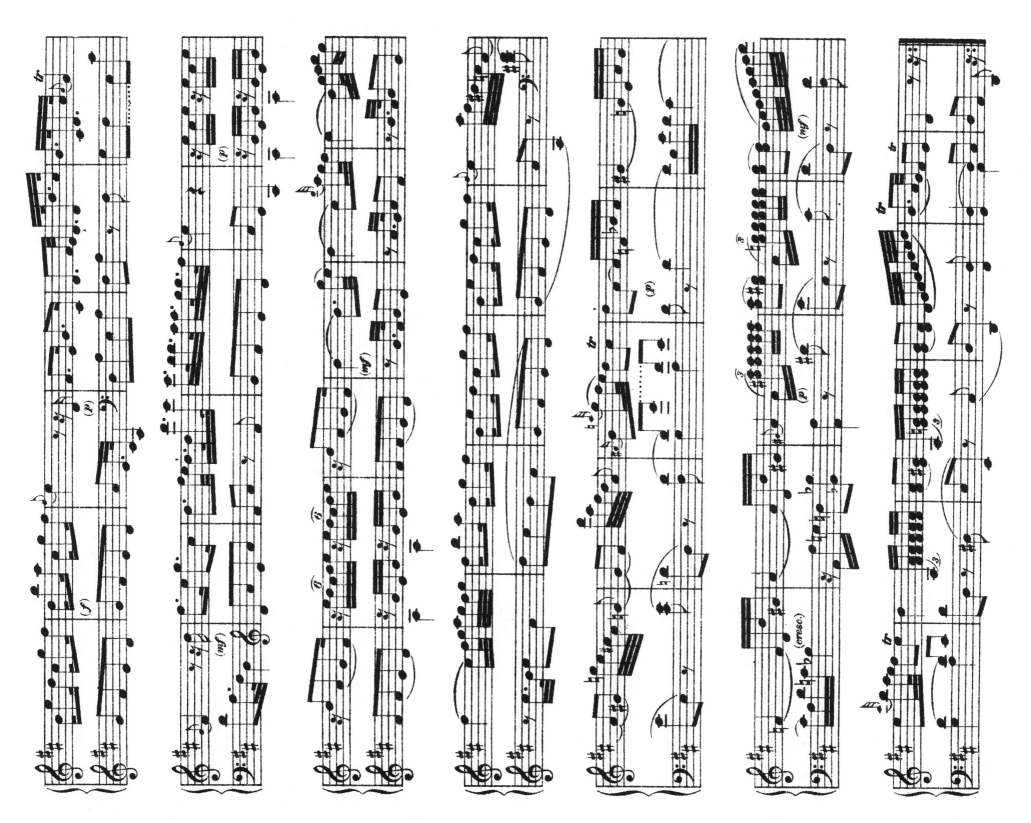

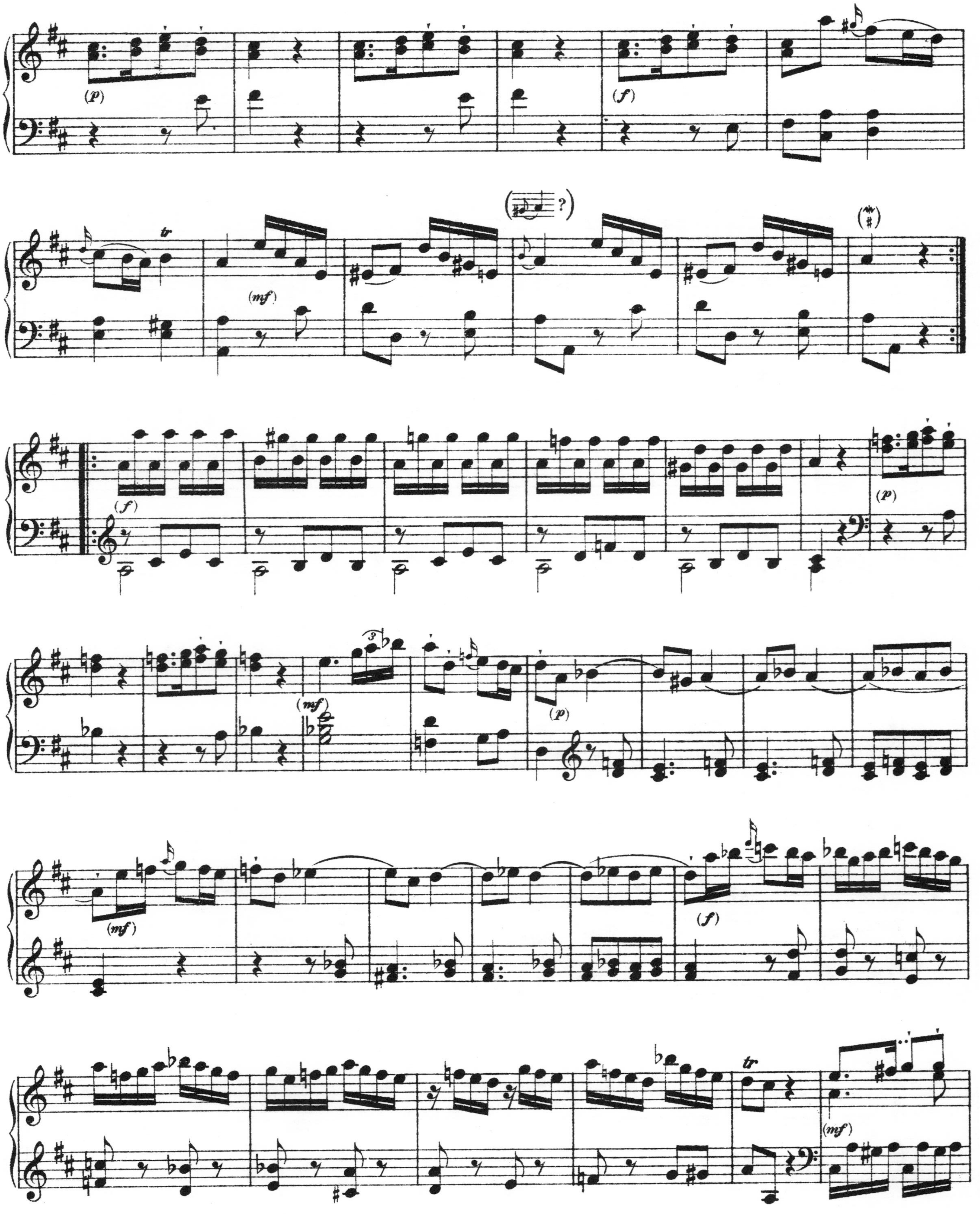
(p)
(f)
tr
(mf)
(p)
(mf)
(p)
(mf)
(f)
tr
(mf)

Sonata No. 15 in C Major

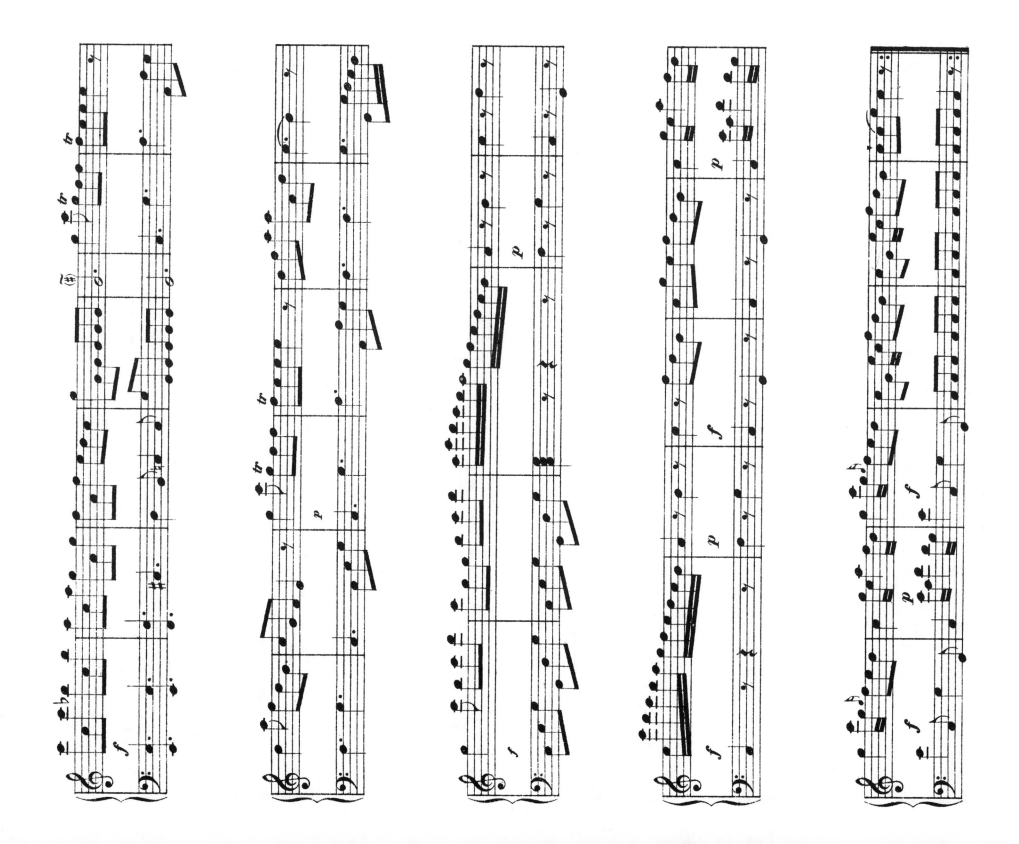

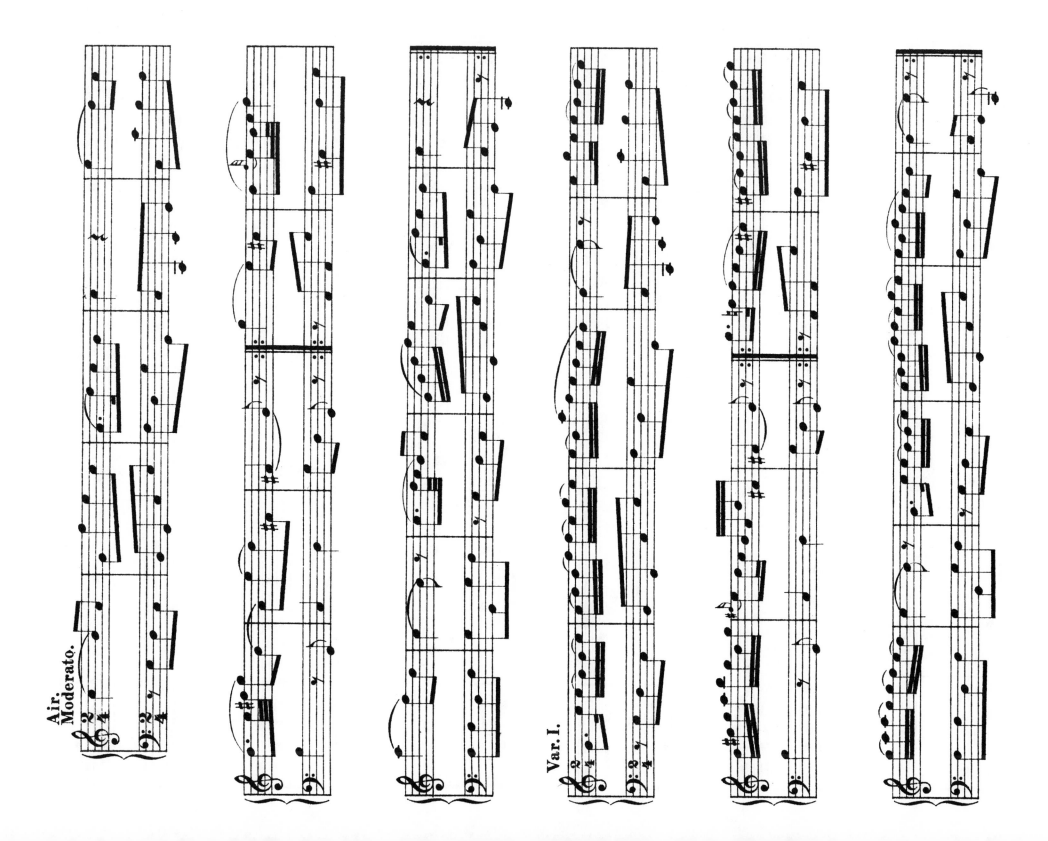

Var. II.

Var. III.

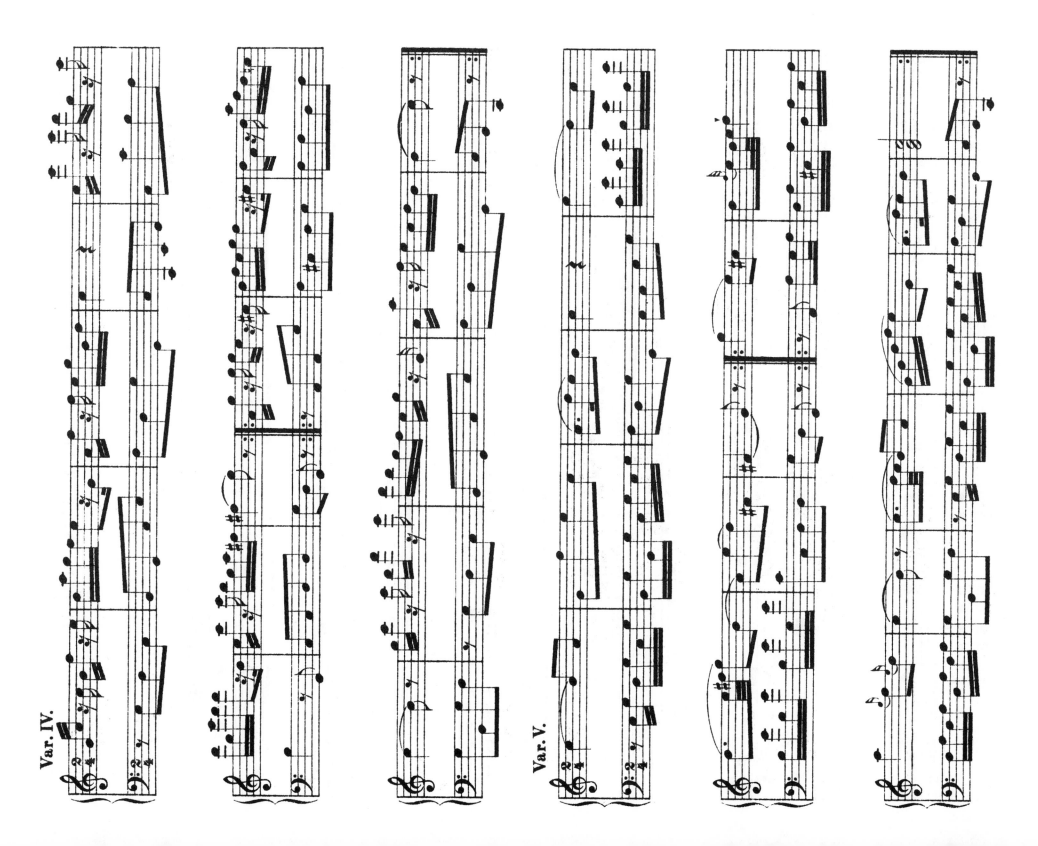

Sonata No. 16 in E-flat Major

Menuet.

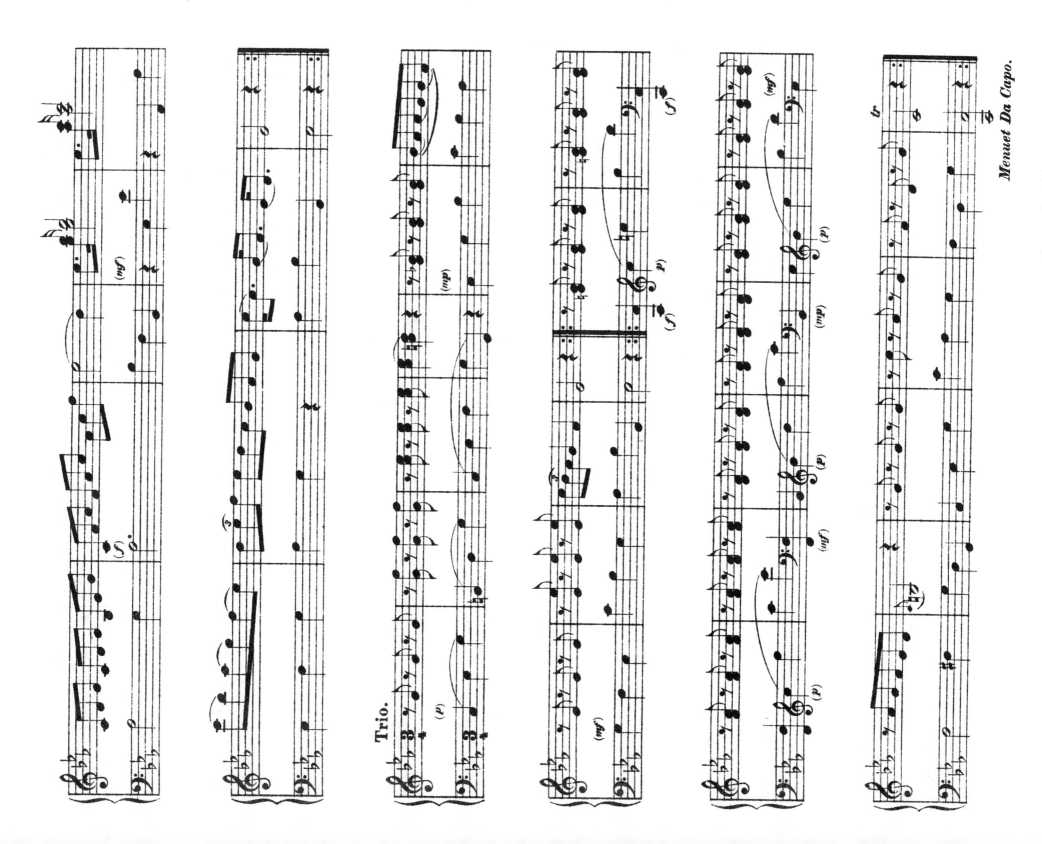

Menuet Da Capo.

Sonata No. 17 in B-flat Major

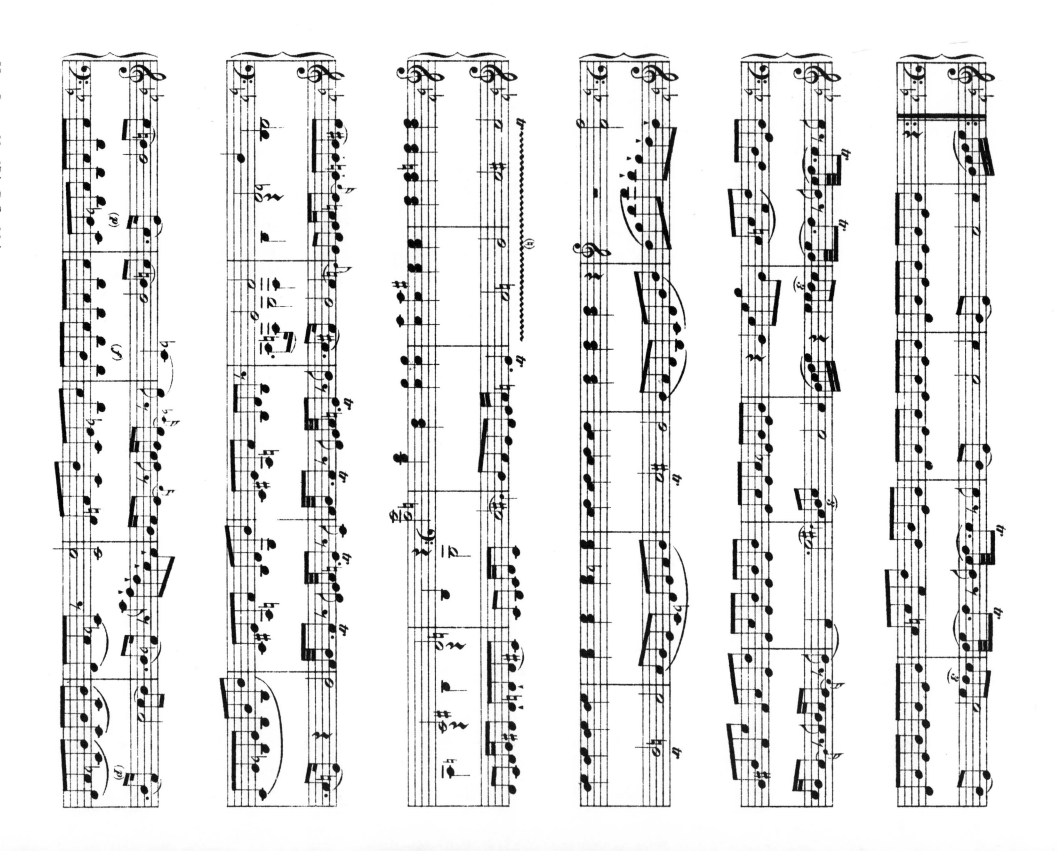

Andante.

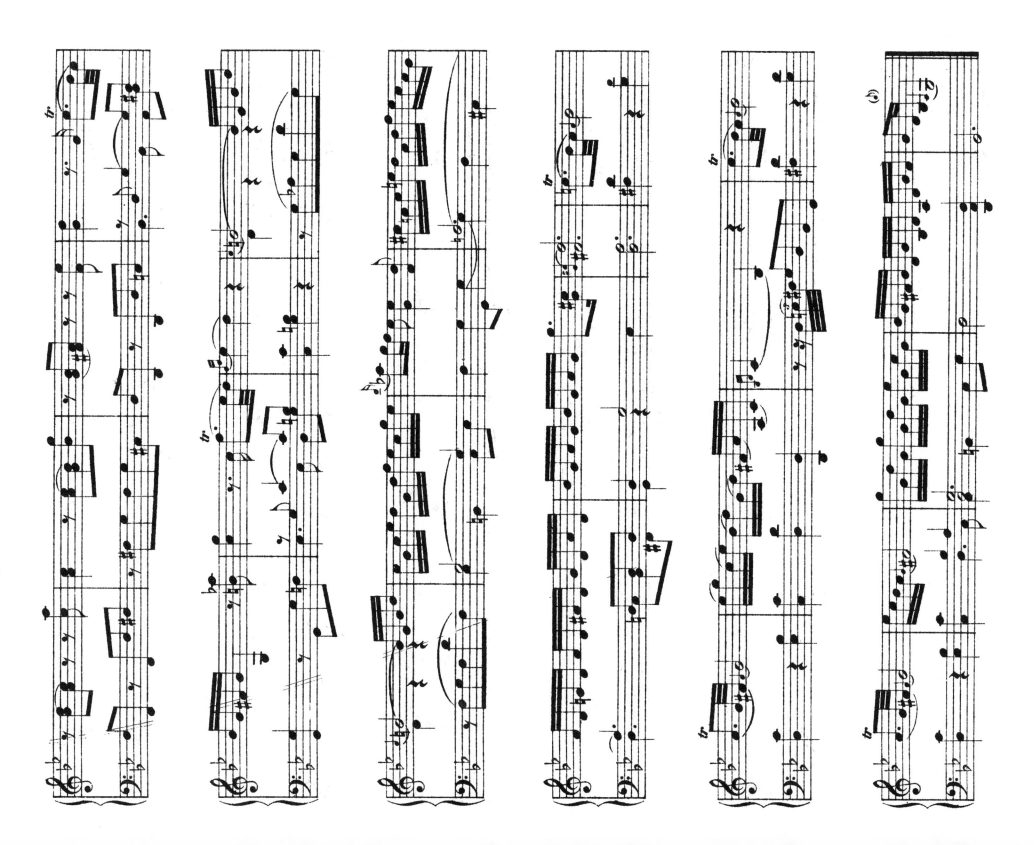

Sonata No. 18 in B-flat Major

Allegro moderato.

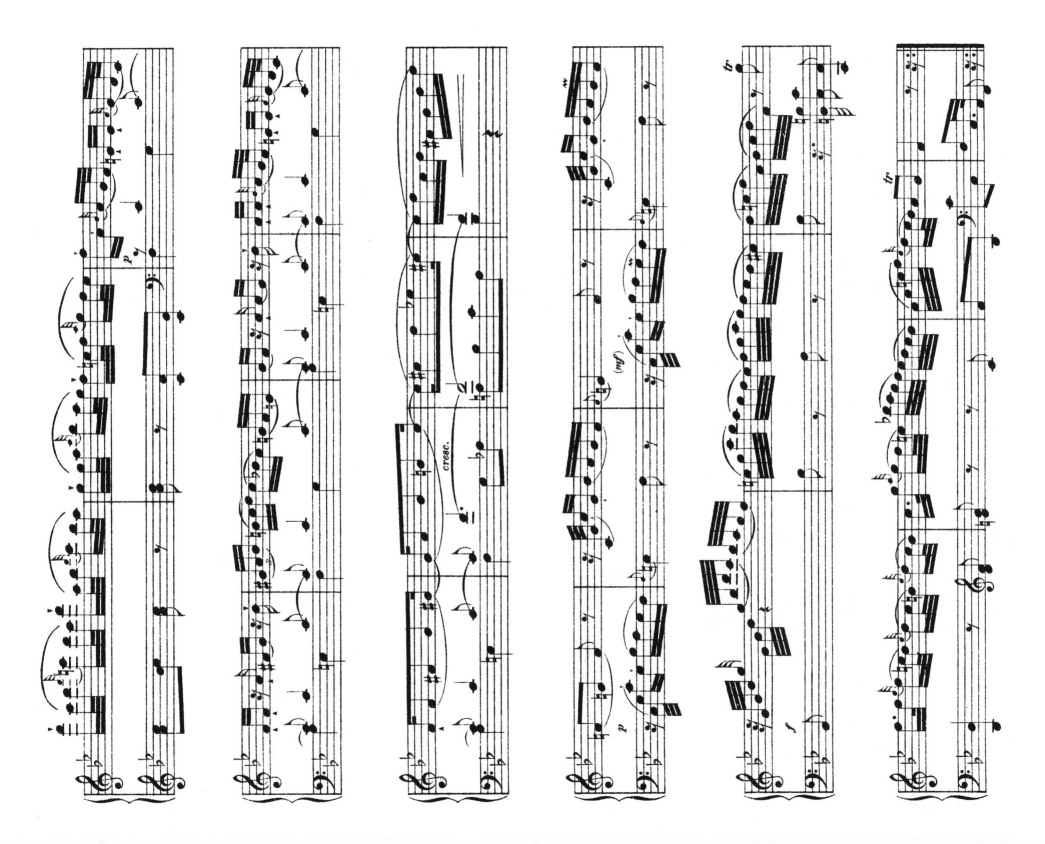

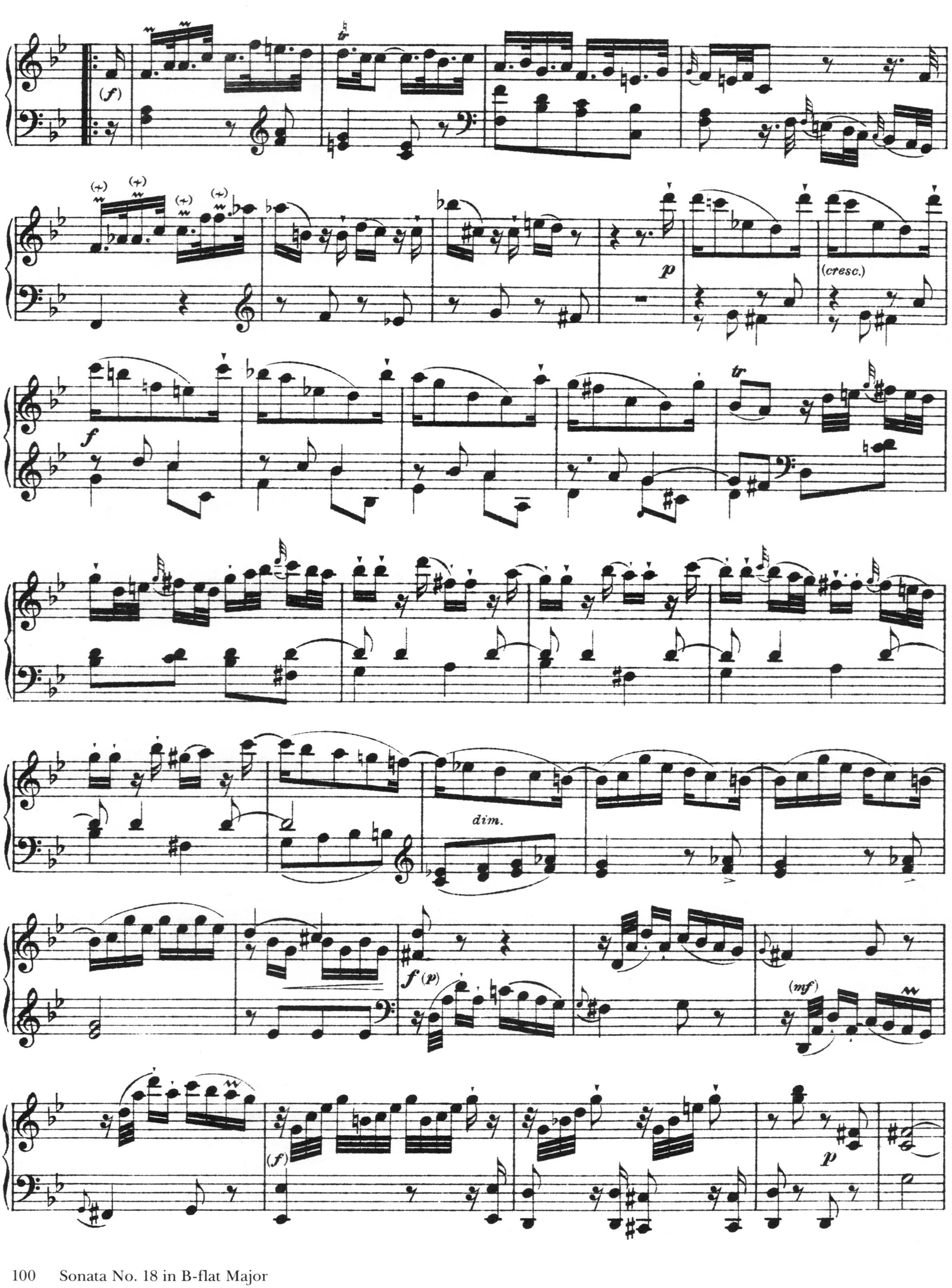
(f)
tr
(+)
p
(cresc.)
f
tr
dim.
f (p)
(mf)
(f)
p

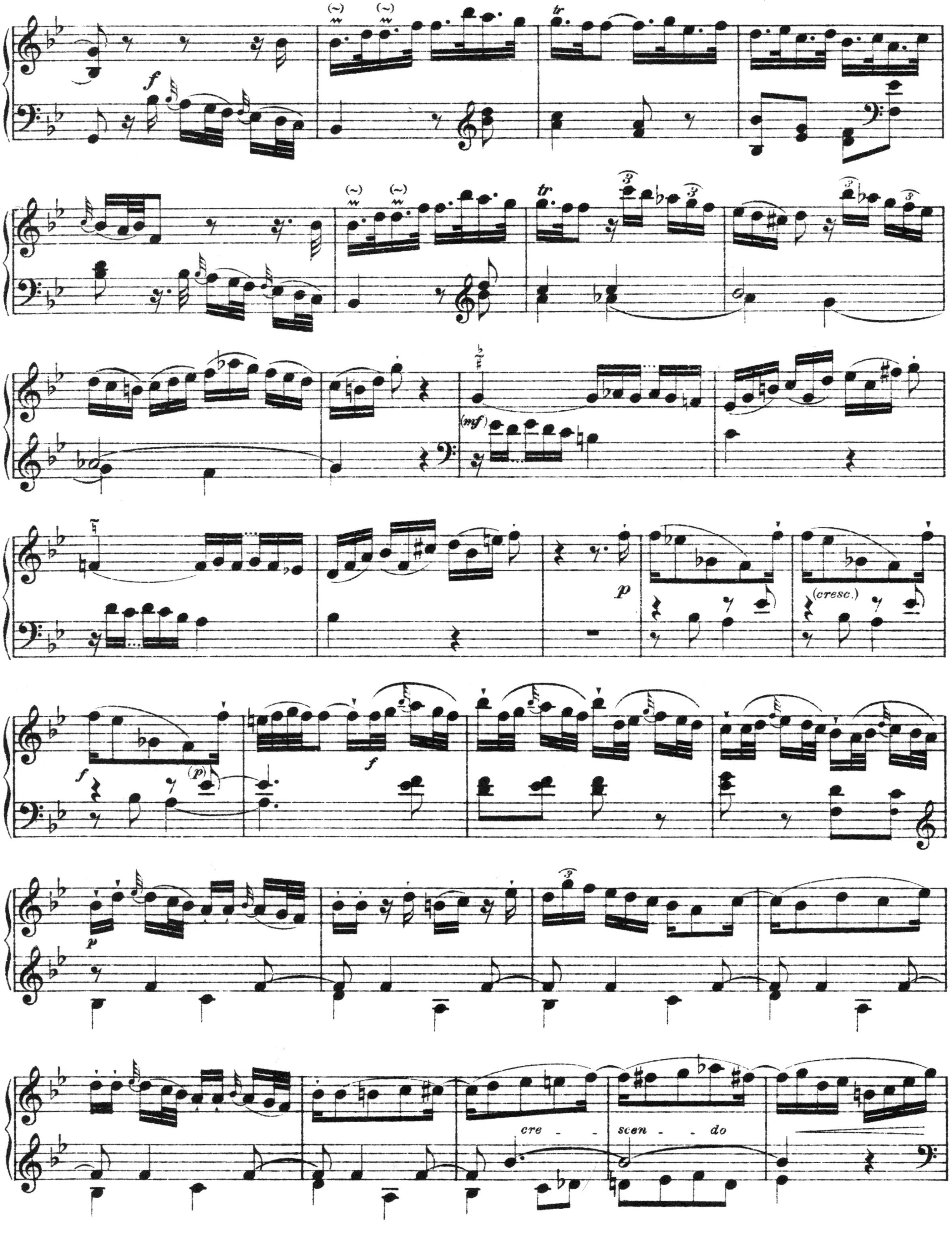
f
tr
tr
(mf)
p
(cresc.)
f
(p)
f
p
cre - - scen - - do

Moderato.

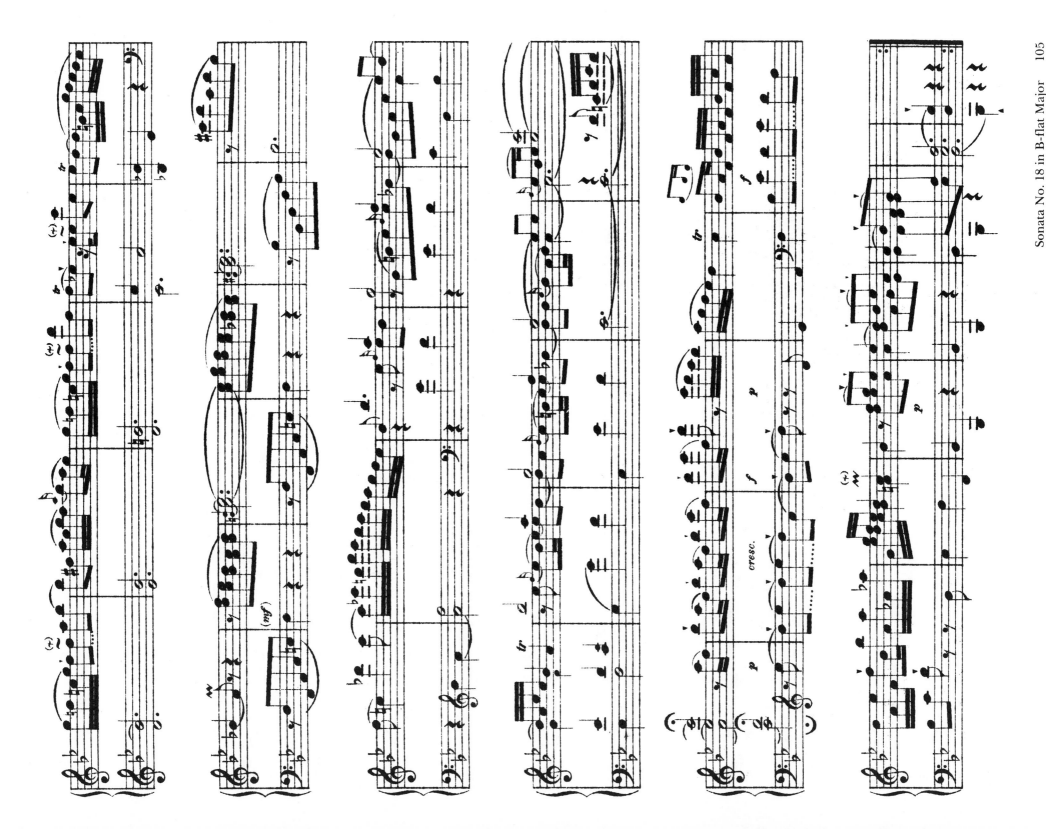

Sonata No. 19 in D Major

Moderato.

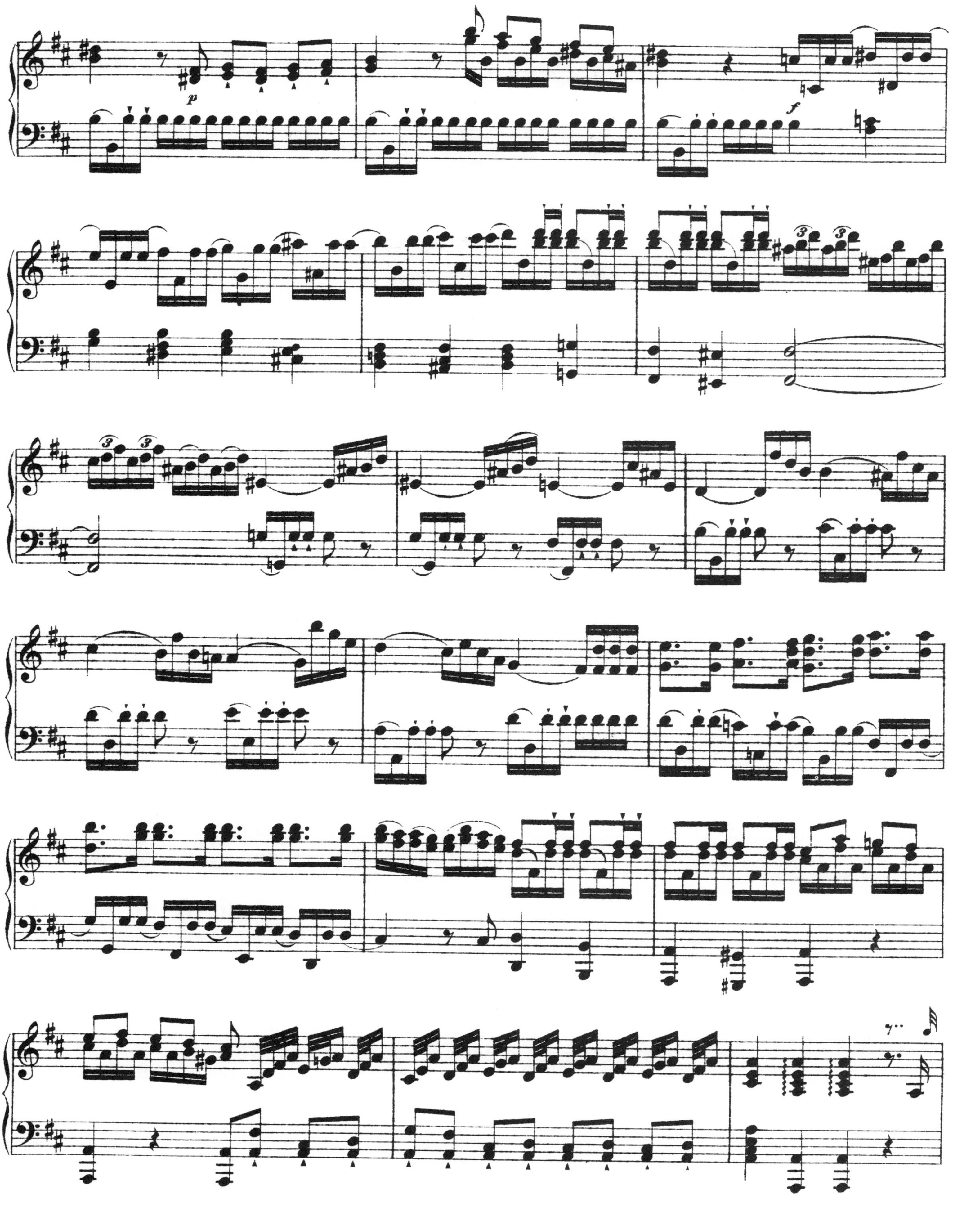
p
f
3
3
3
3

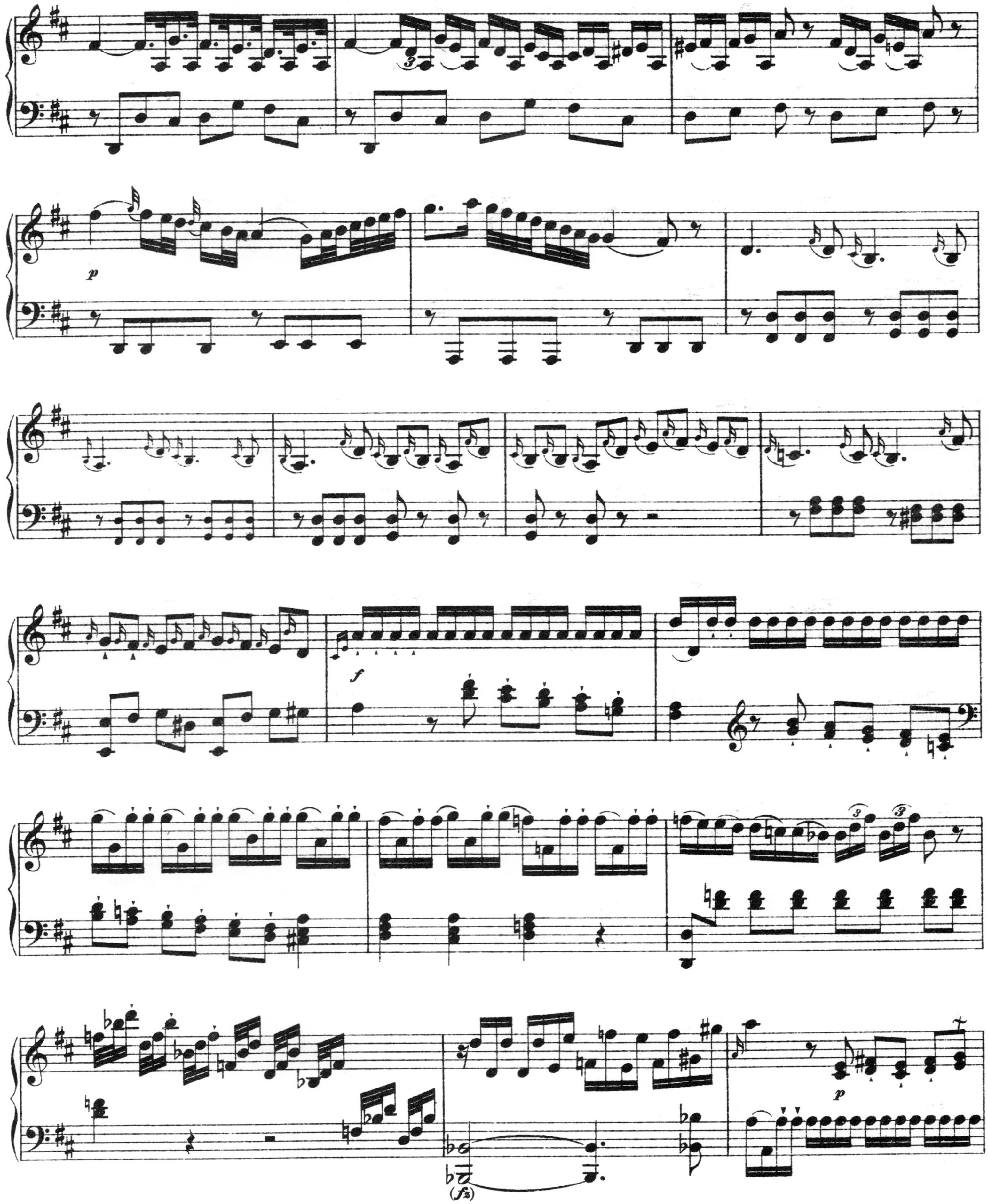
p
p
f
(fz)
p

Adagio, ma non troppo.

Andante.

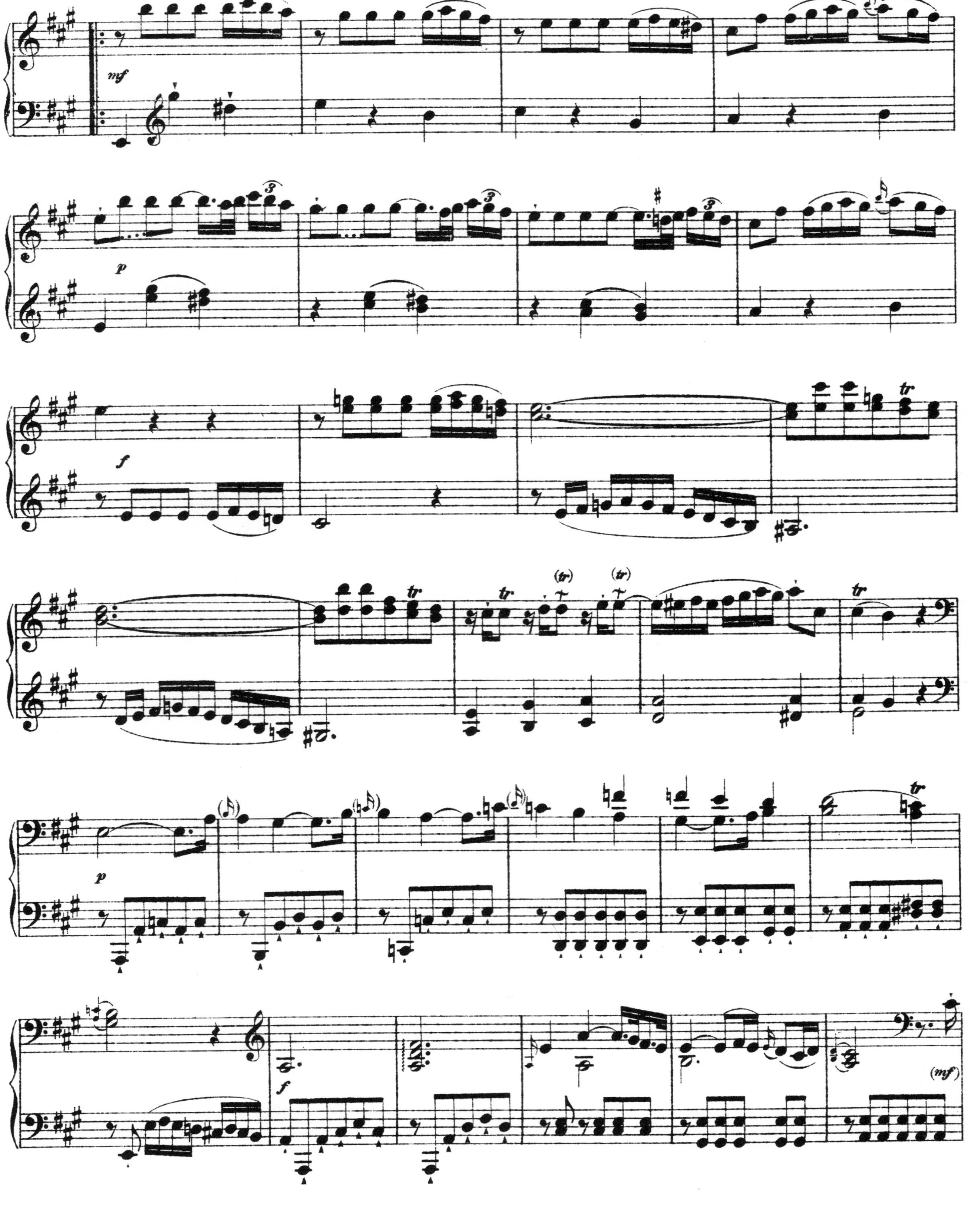
mf
p
3
f
tr
(tr)
(mf)

Finale.
Allegro assai.

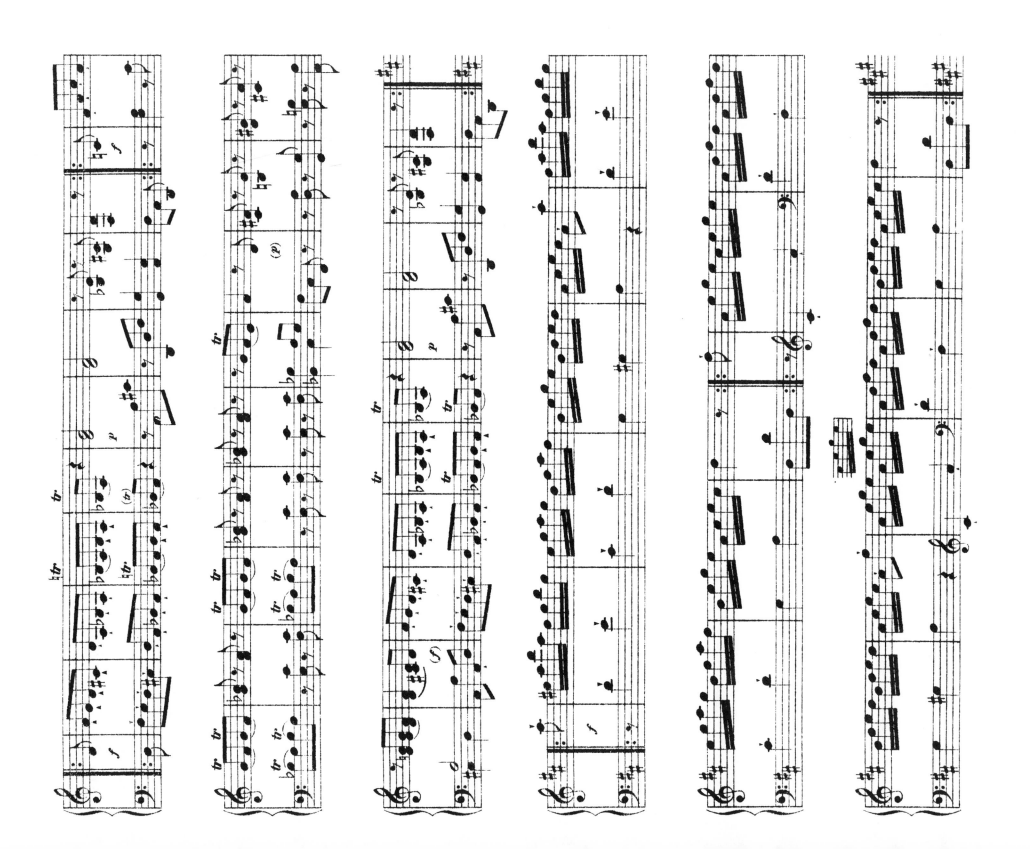

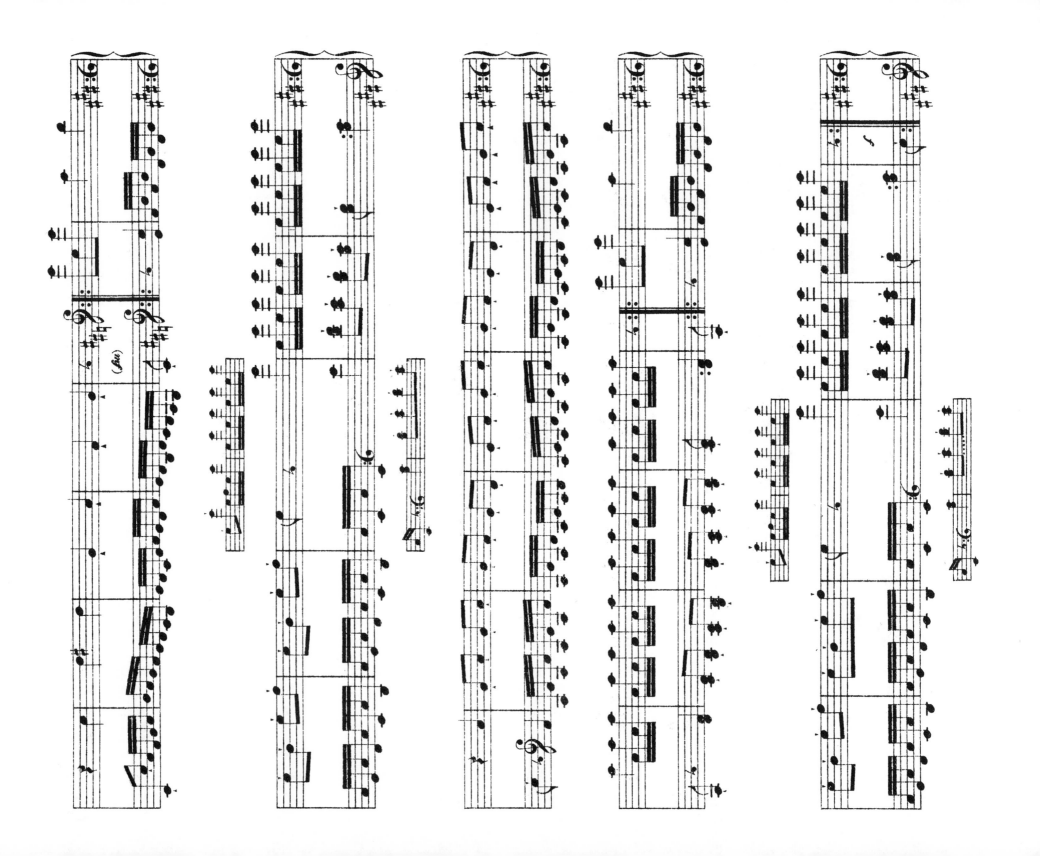

Sonata No. 20 in C Minor

Allegro moderato.
Moderato.

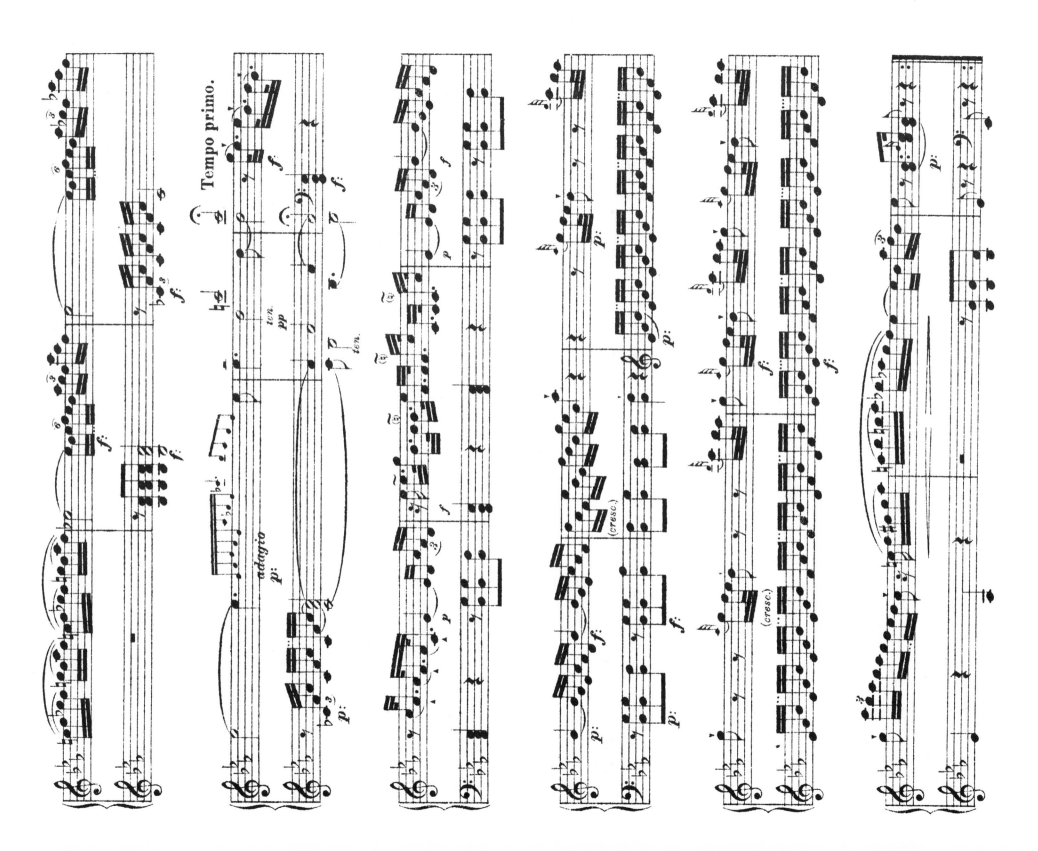

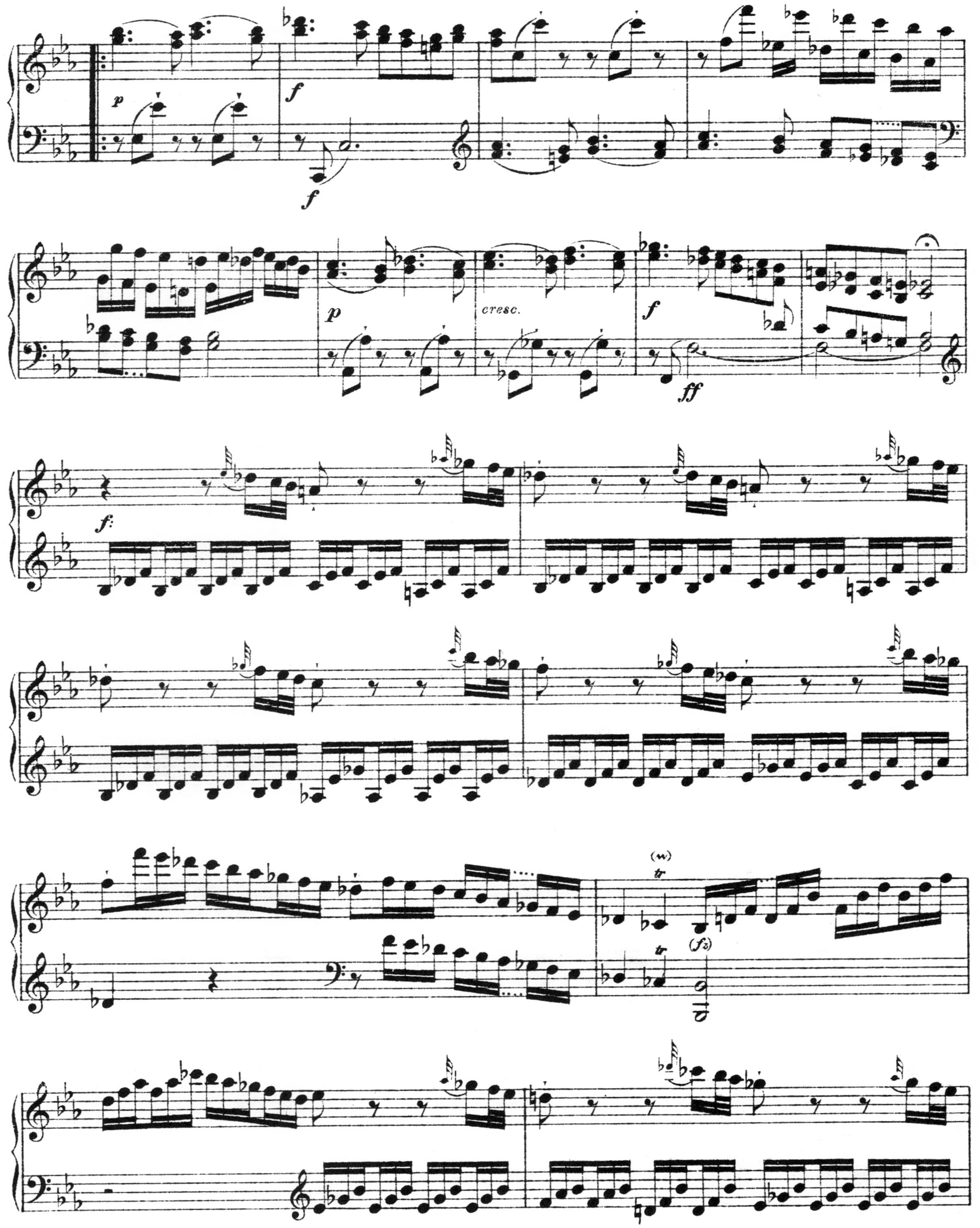
p
f
f
p
cresc.
f
ff
f:
tr
(w)
(fz)

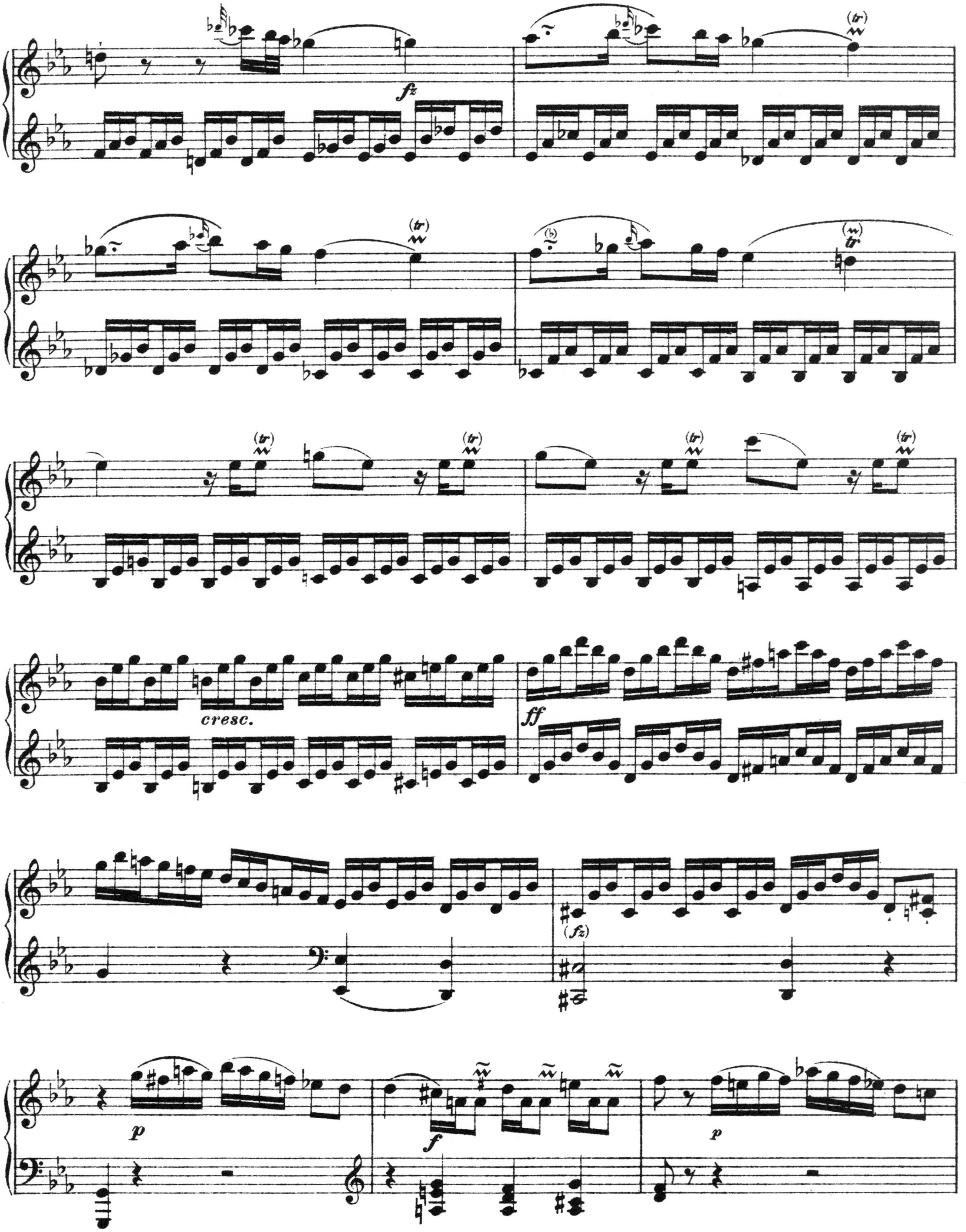
fz
(tr)
cresc.
ff
(fz)
p
f

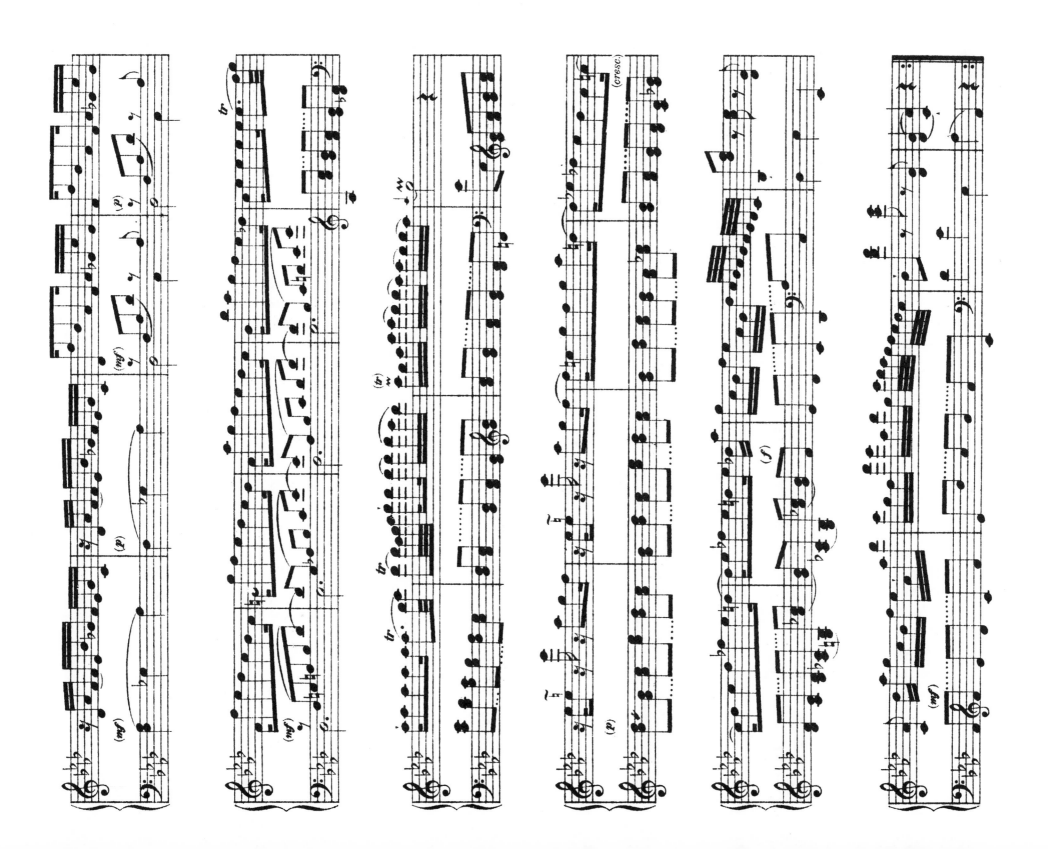

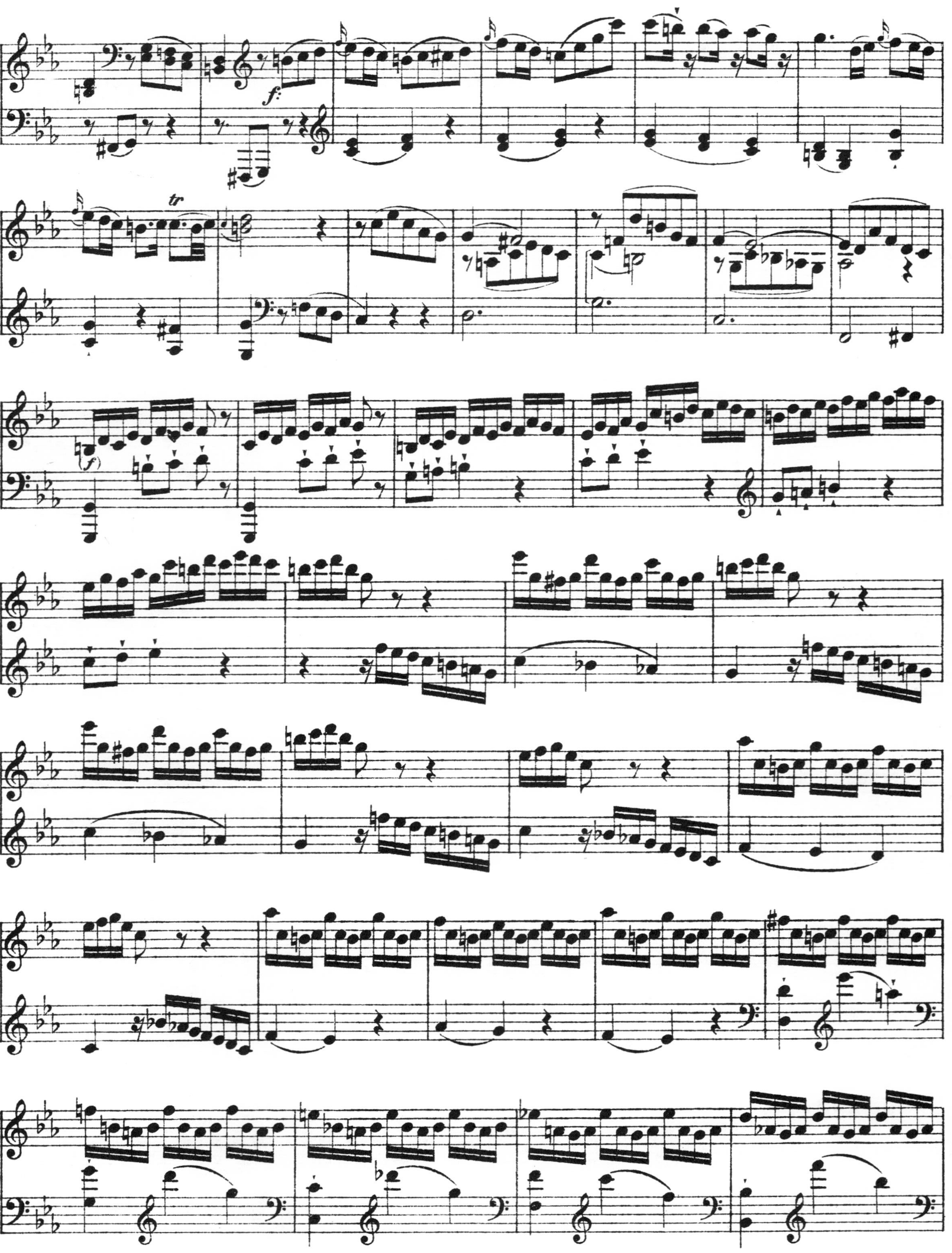

f
tr
(f)

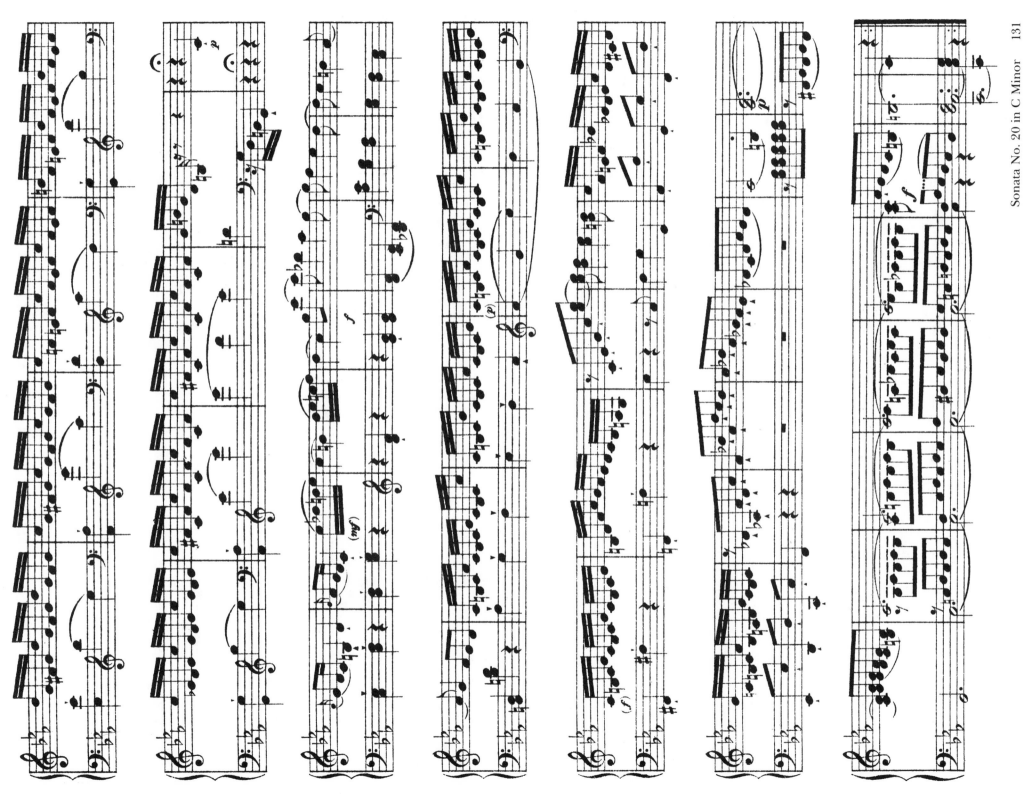

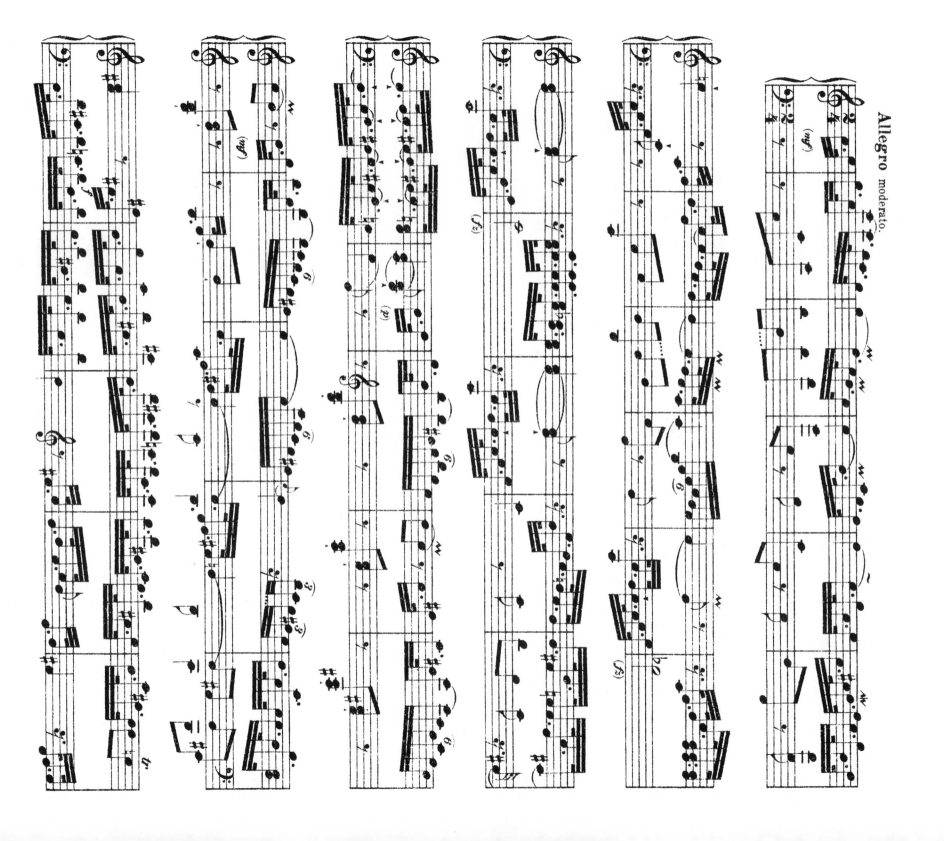

Sonata No. 21 in C Major

Allegro moderato.

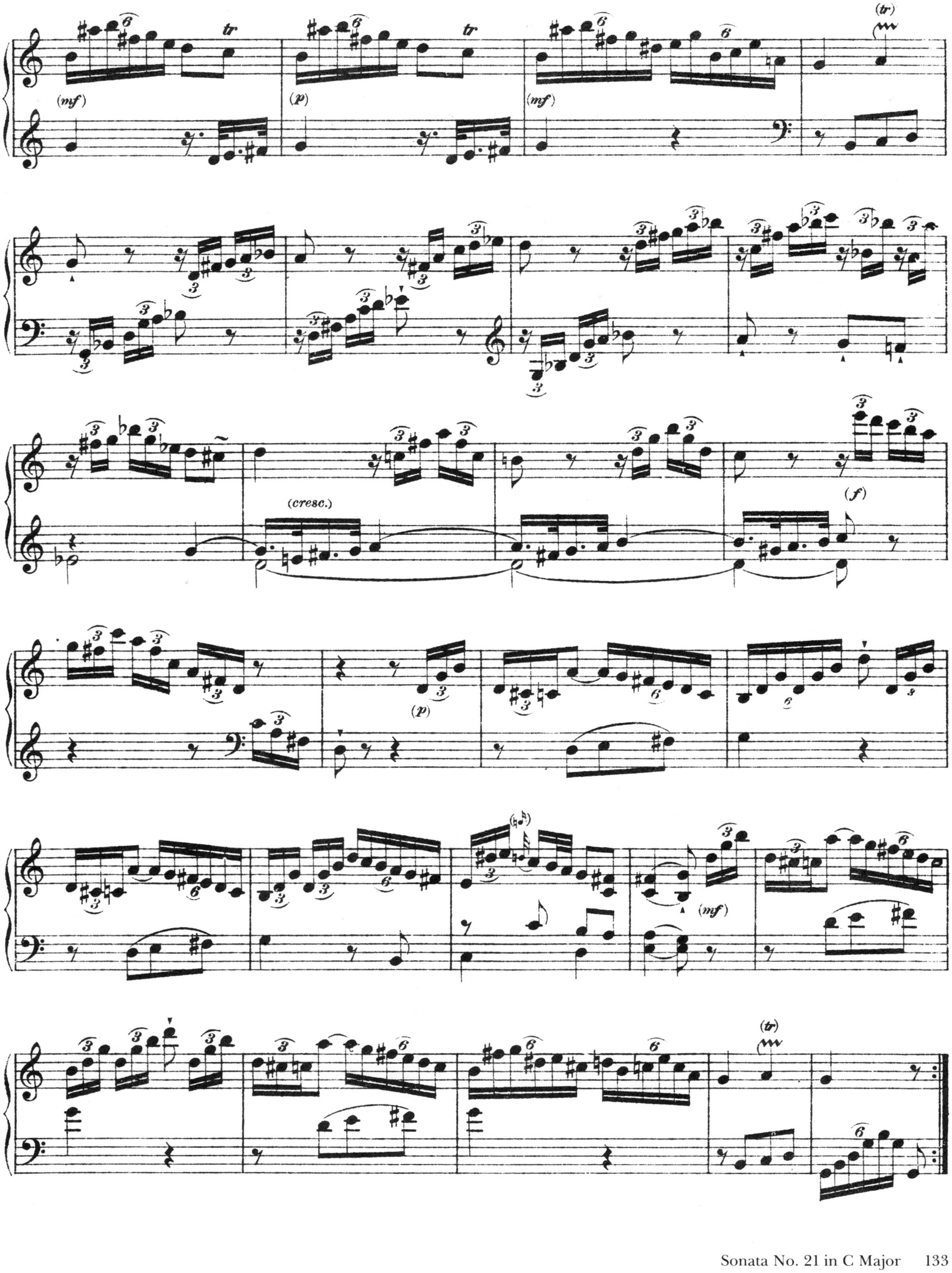

tr
(mf)
(p)
(cresc.)
(f)

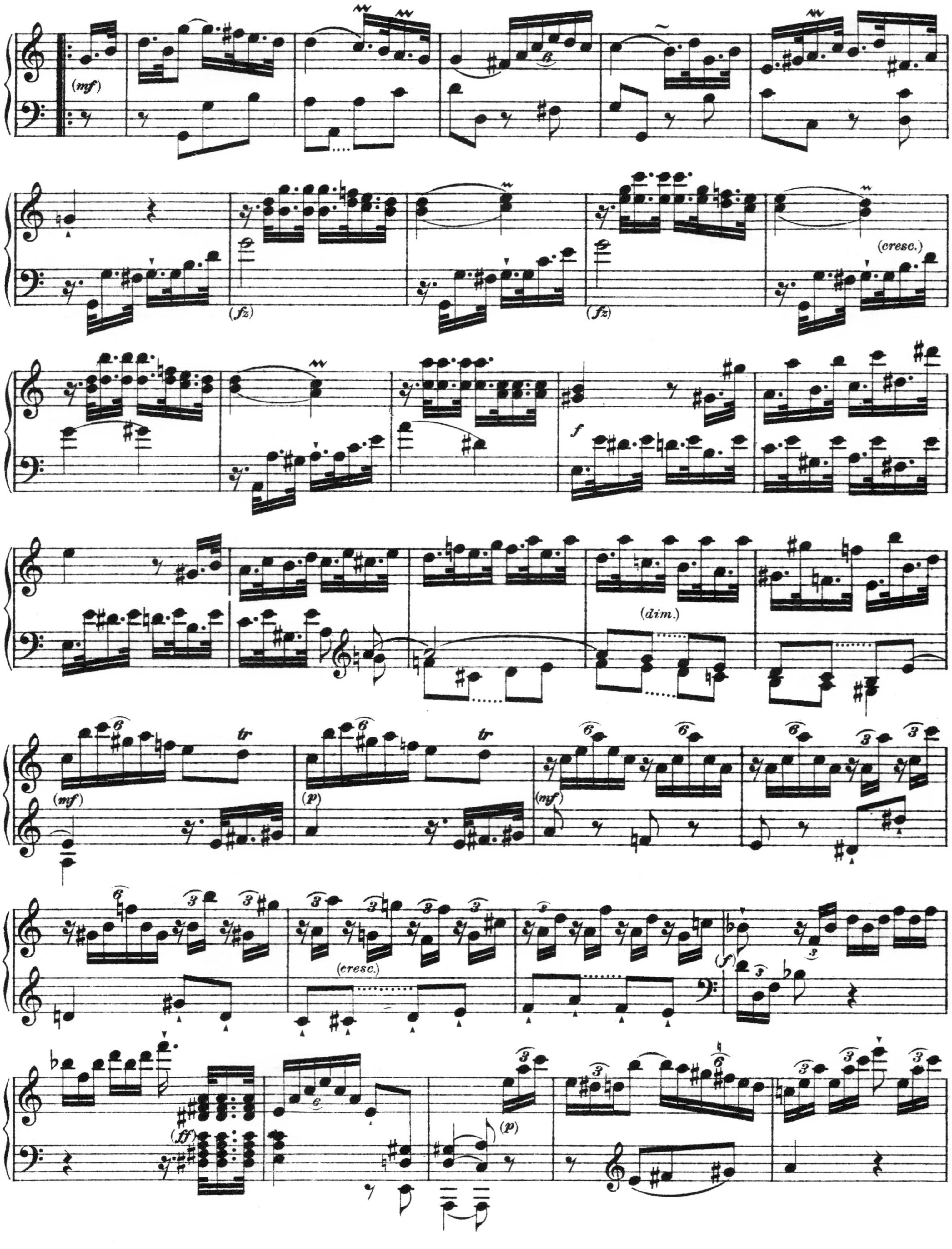
(mf)
(fz)
(fz)
(cresc.)
f
(dim.)
tr
tr
(mf)
(p)
(mf)
(cresc.)
(f)
(ff)
(p)

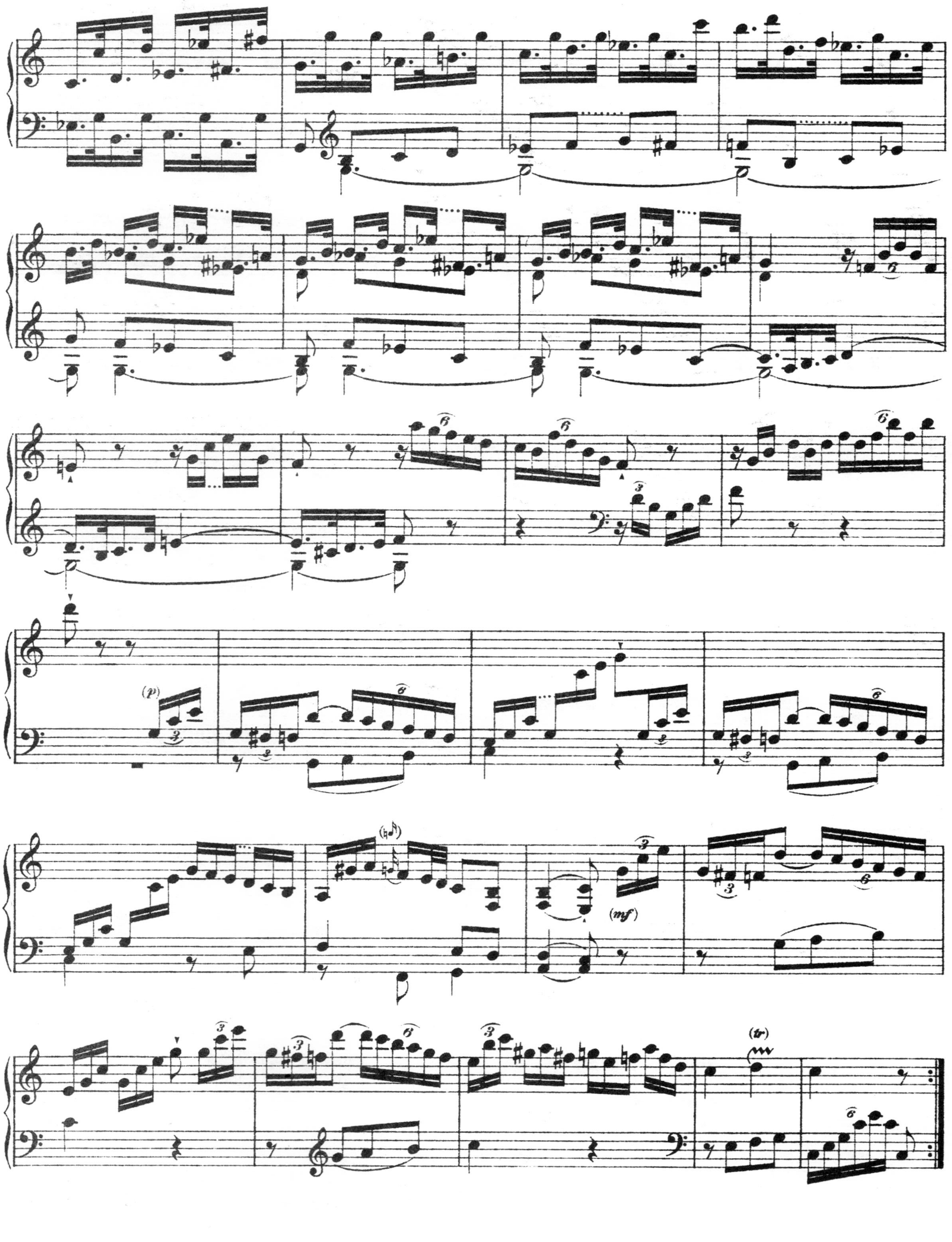
(p)
(mf)
(tr)

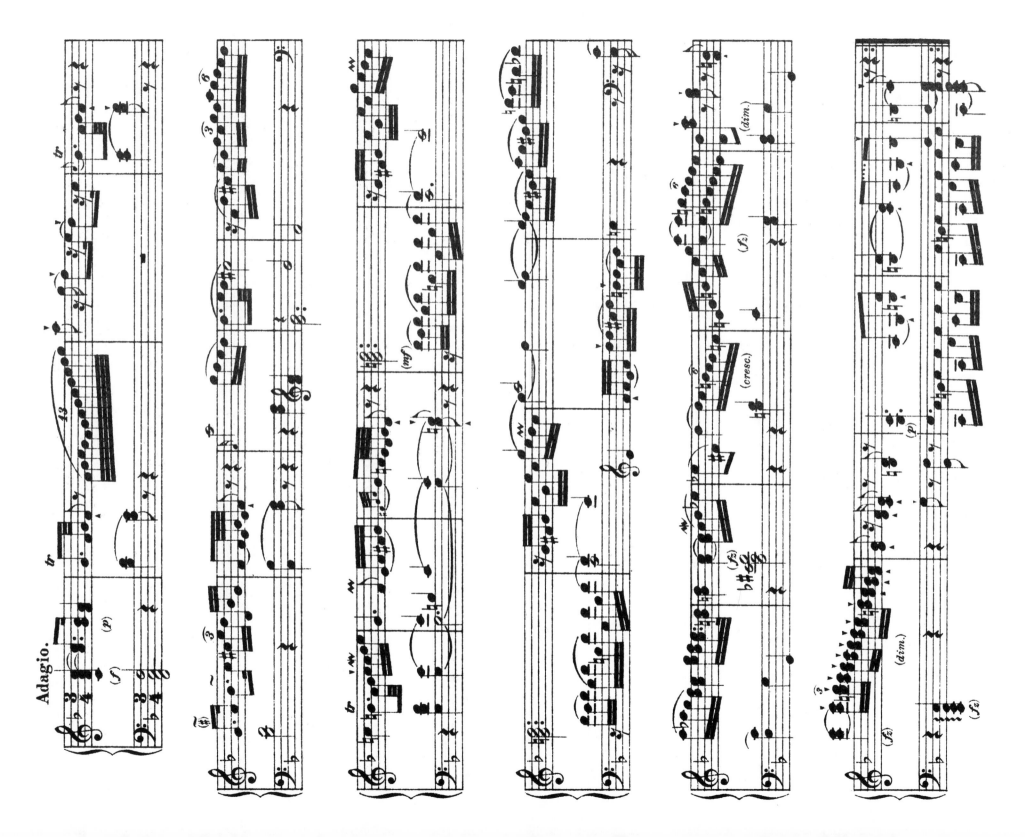

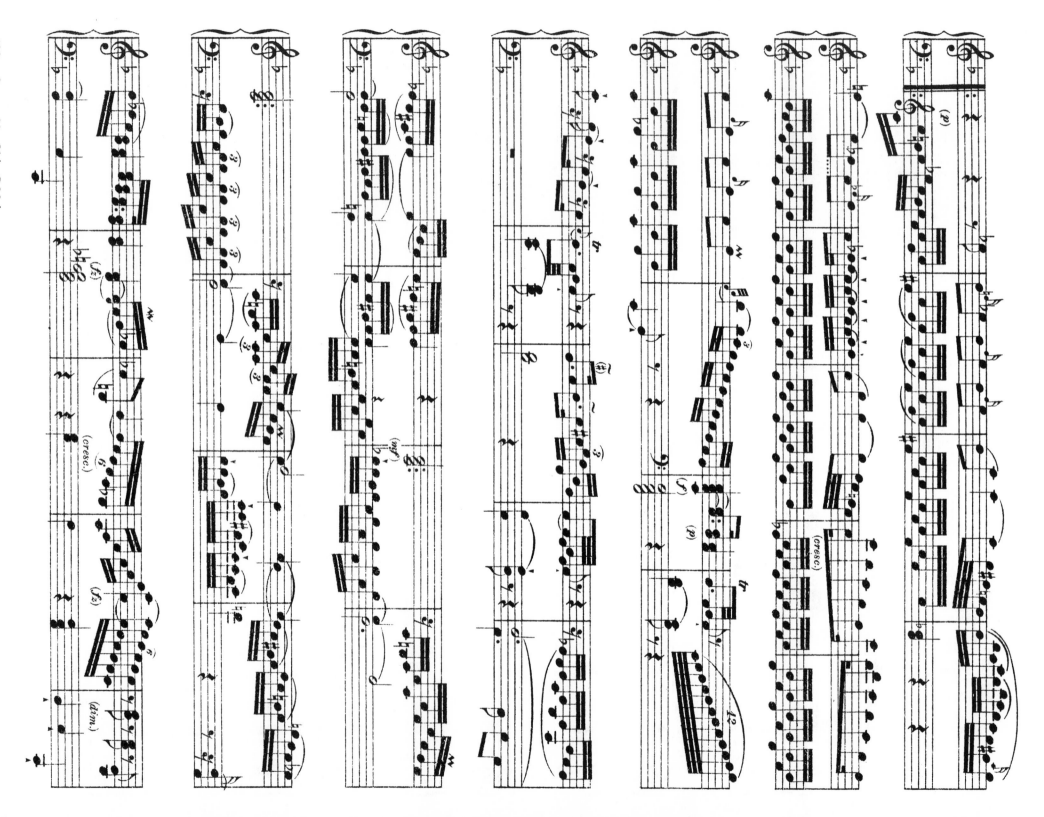

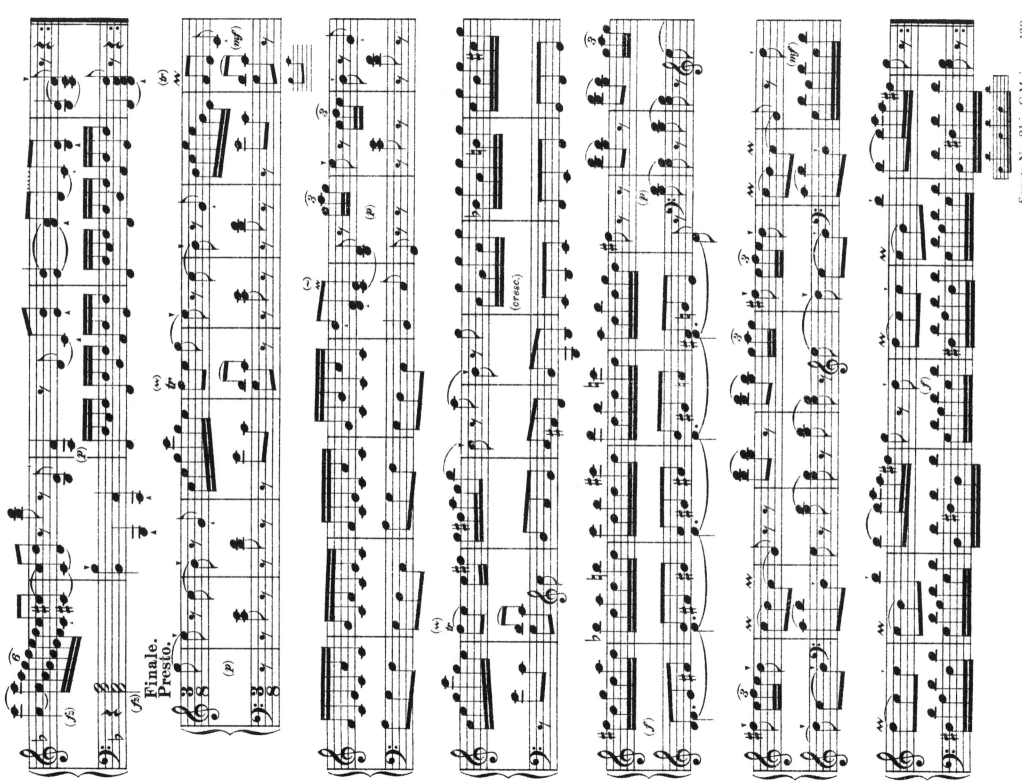

Sonata No. 21 in C Major   139

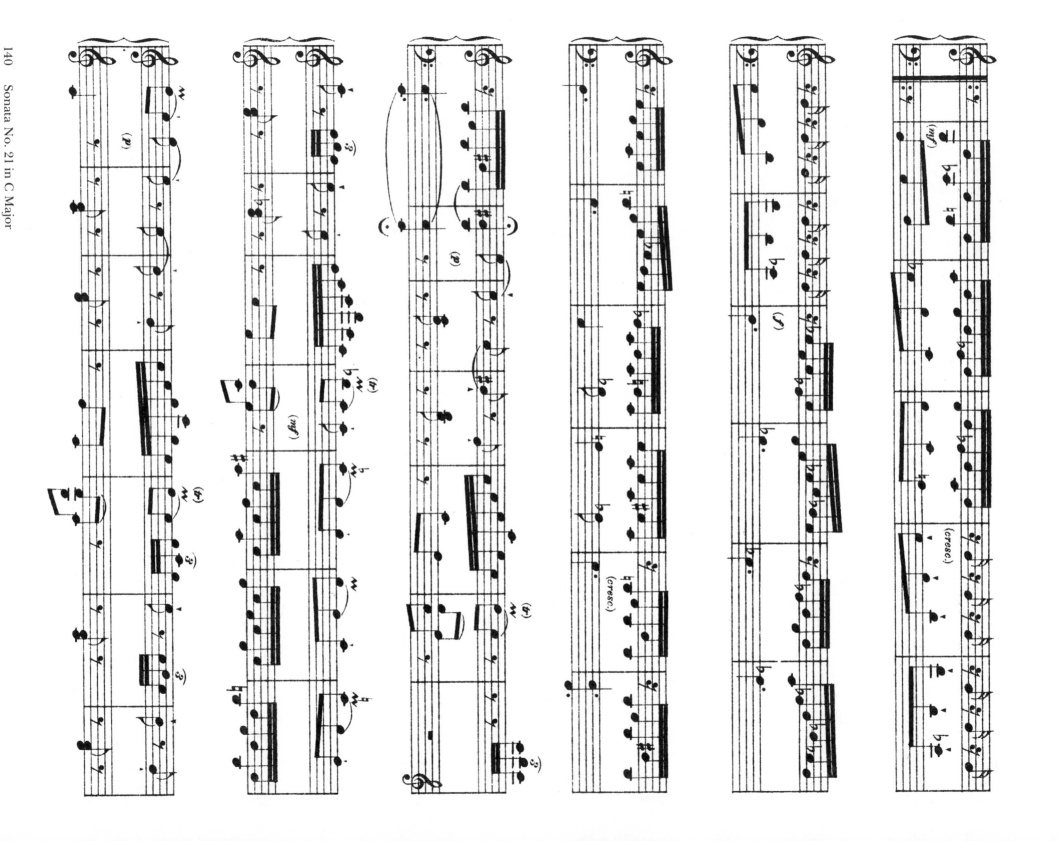

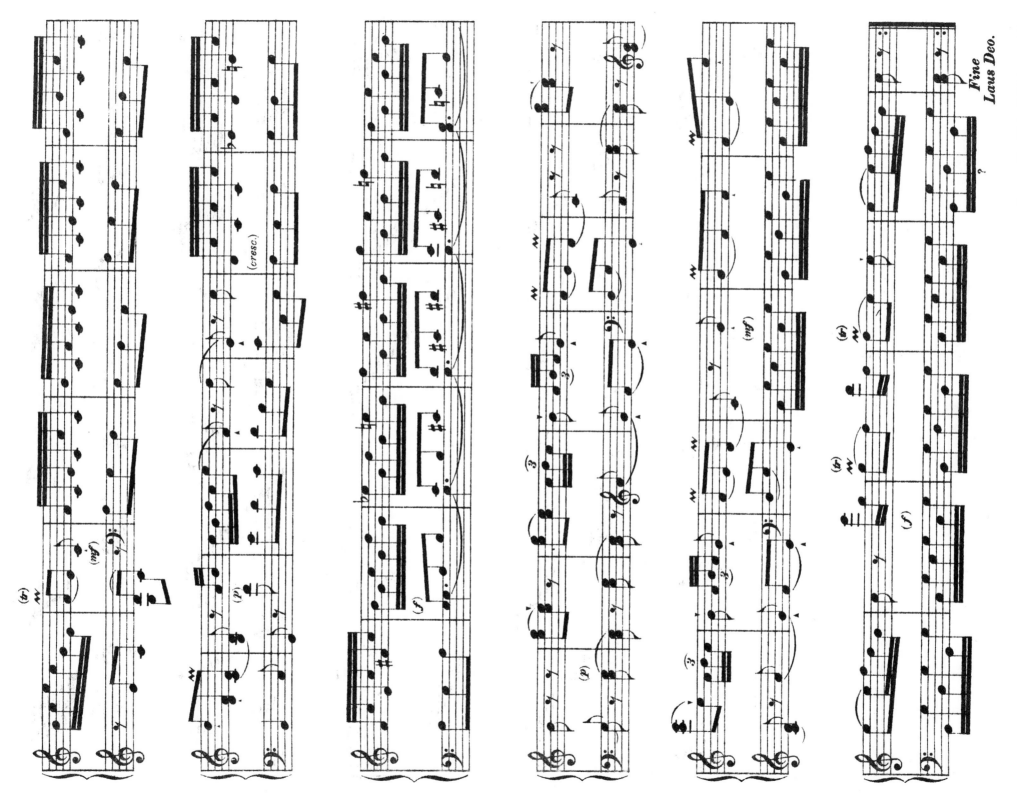

Fine
Laus Deo.

Sonata No. 22 in E Major

Allegro moderato.

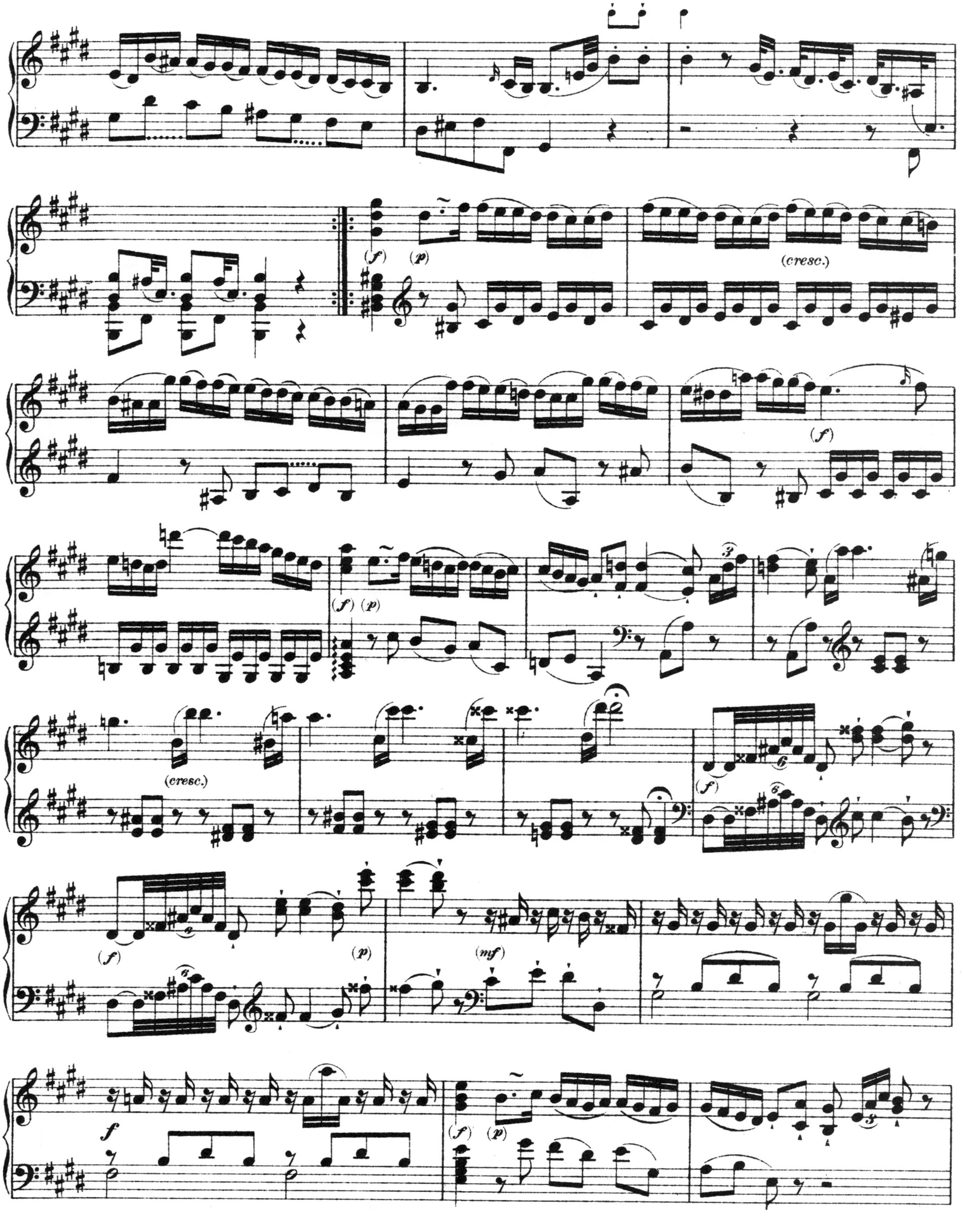
(f)
(p)
(cresc.)
(f)
(f)
(p)
(cresc.)
(f)
(f)
(p)
(mf)
f
(f)
(p)

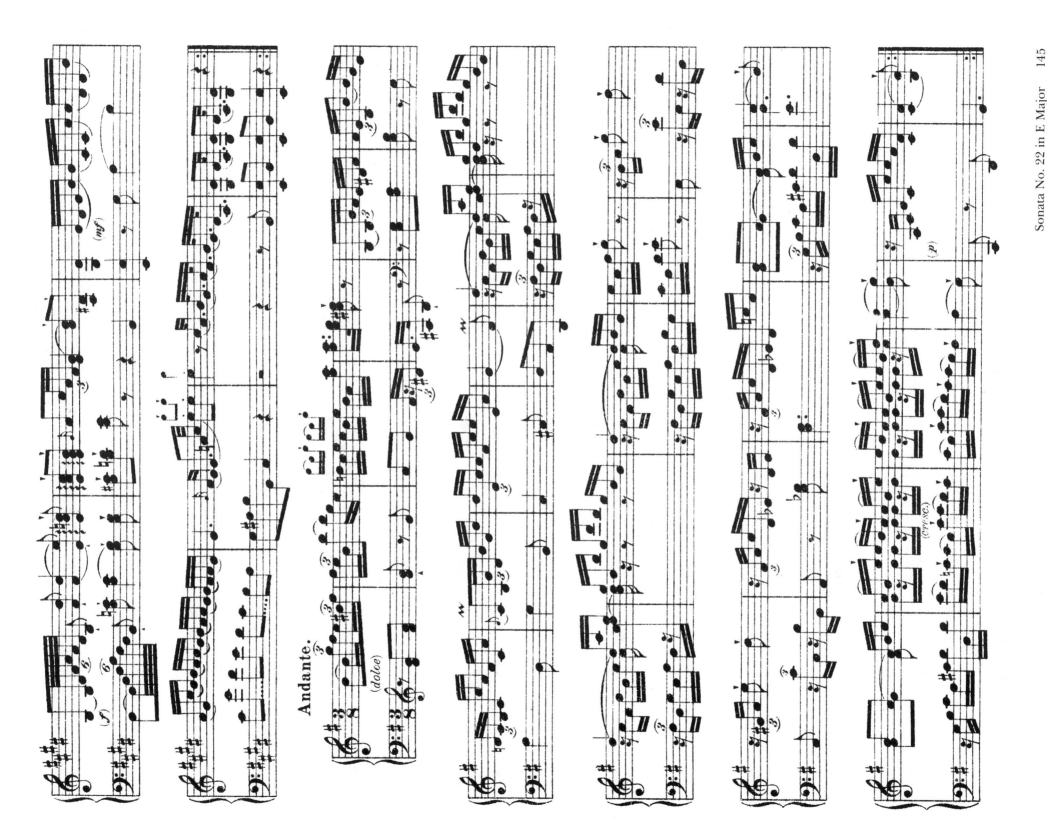

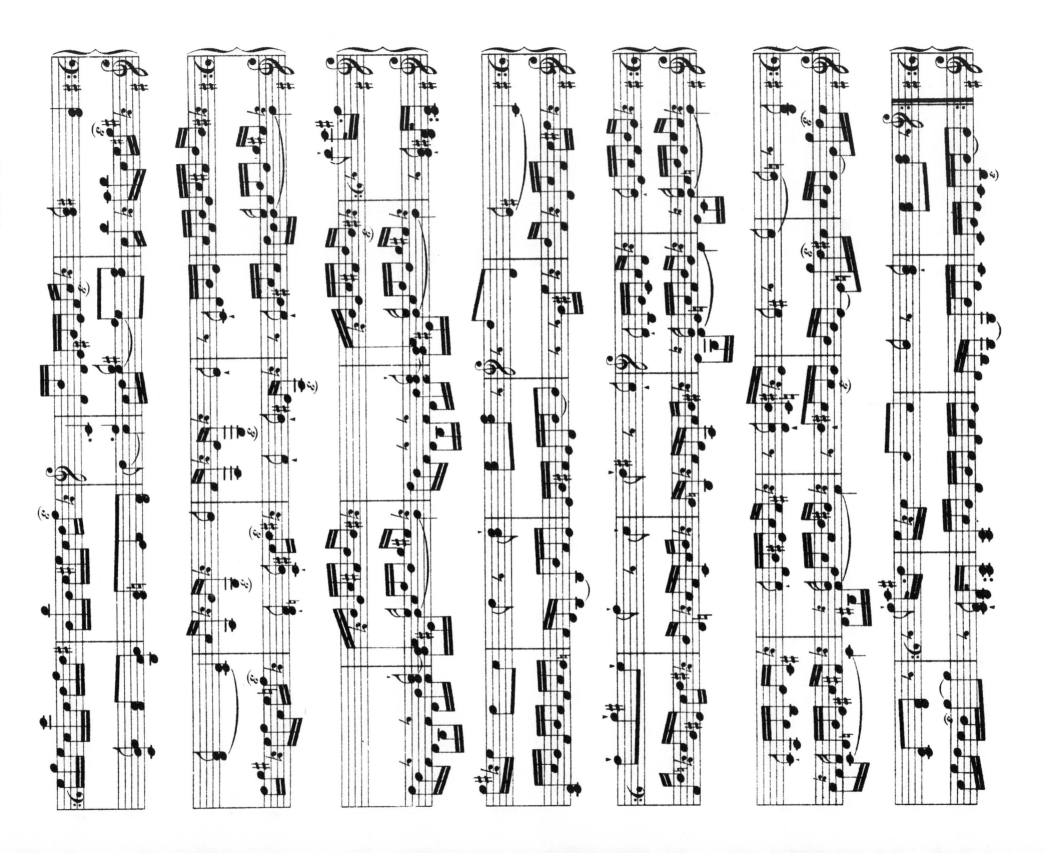

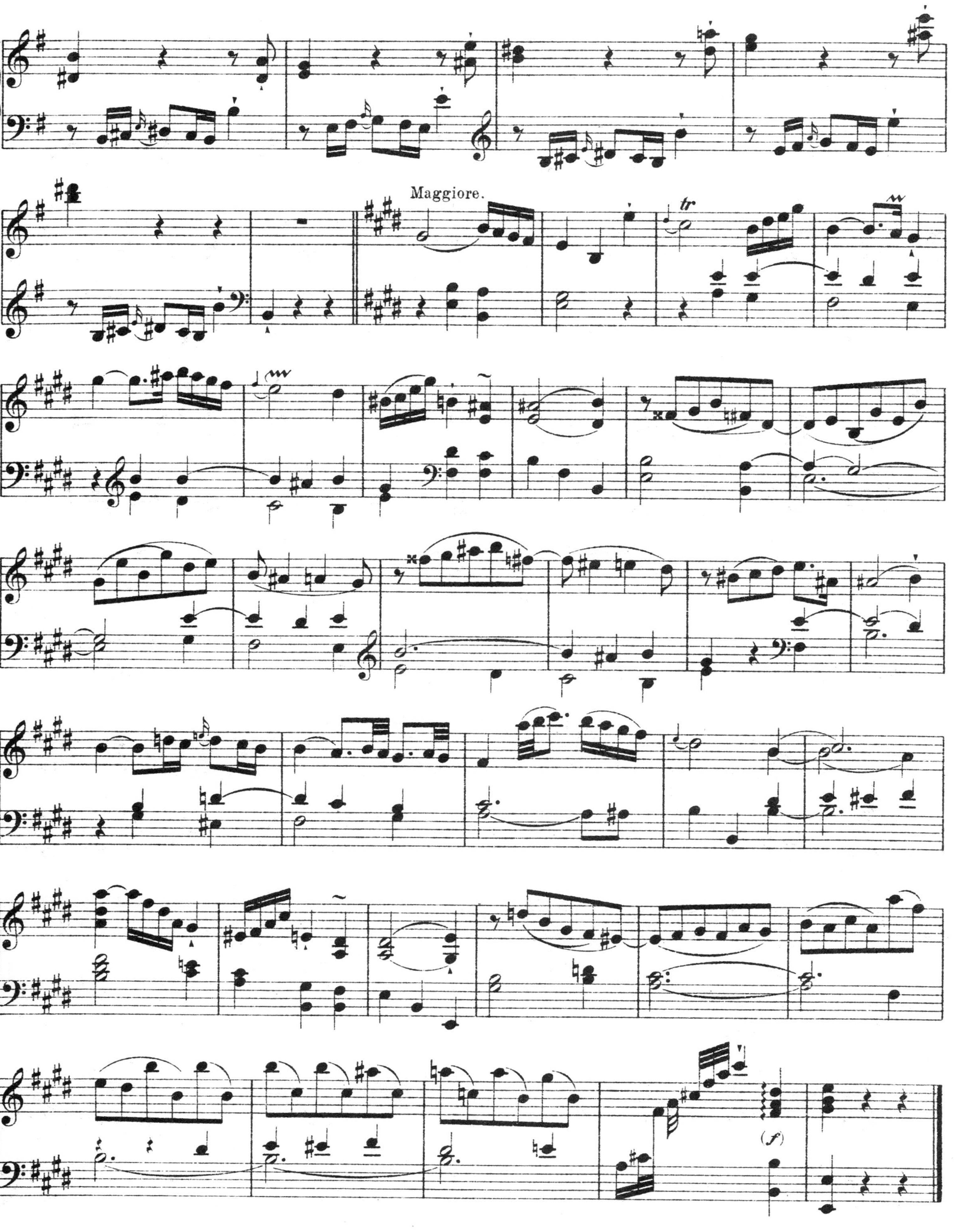
Maggiore.
tr
(f)

Sonata No. 23 in F Major

Allegro moderato.

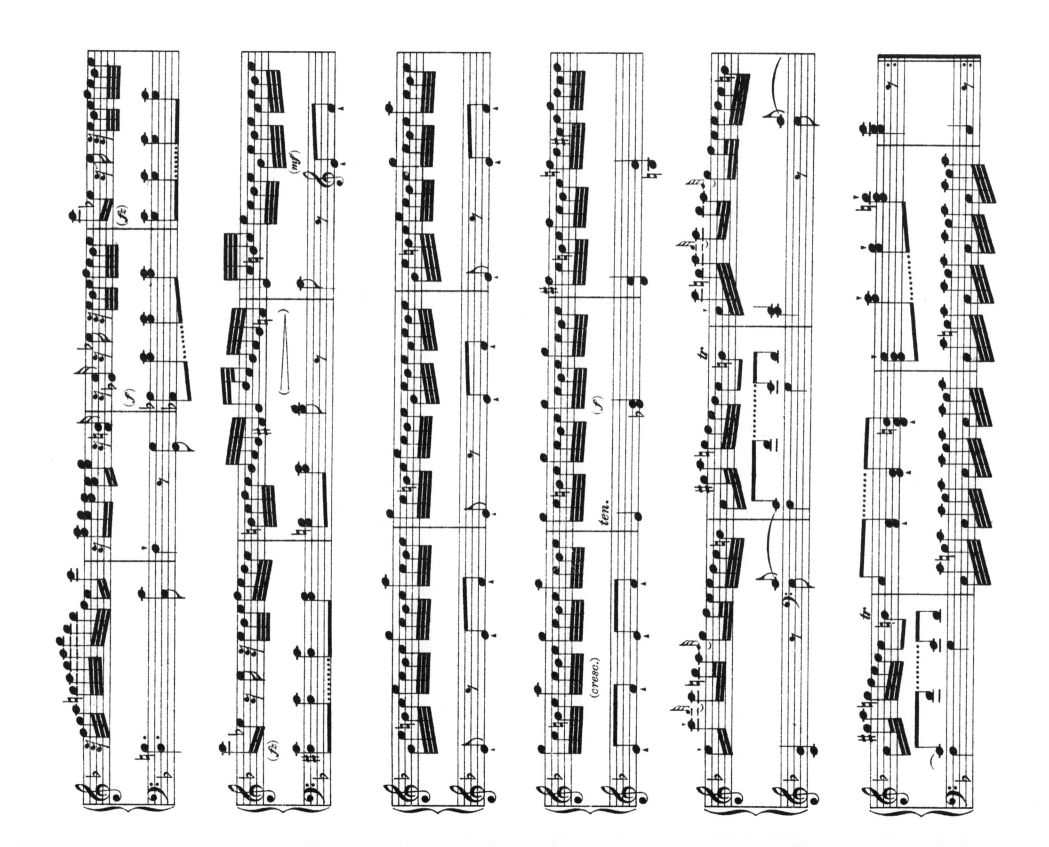

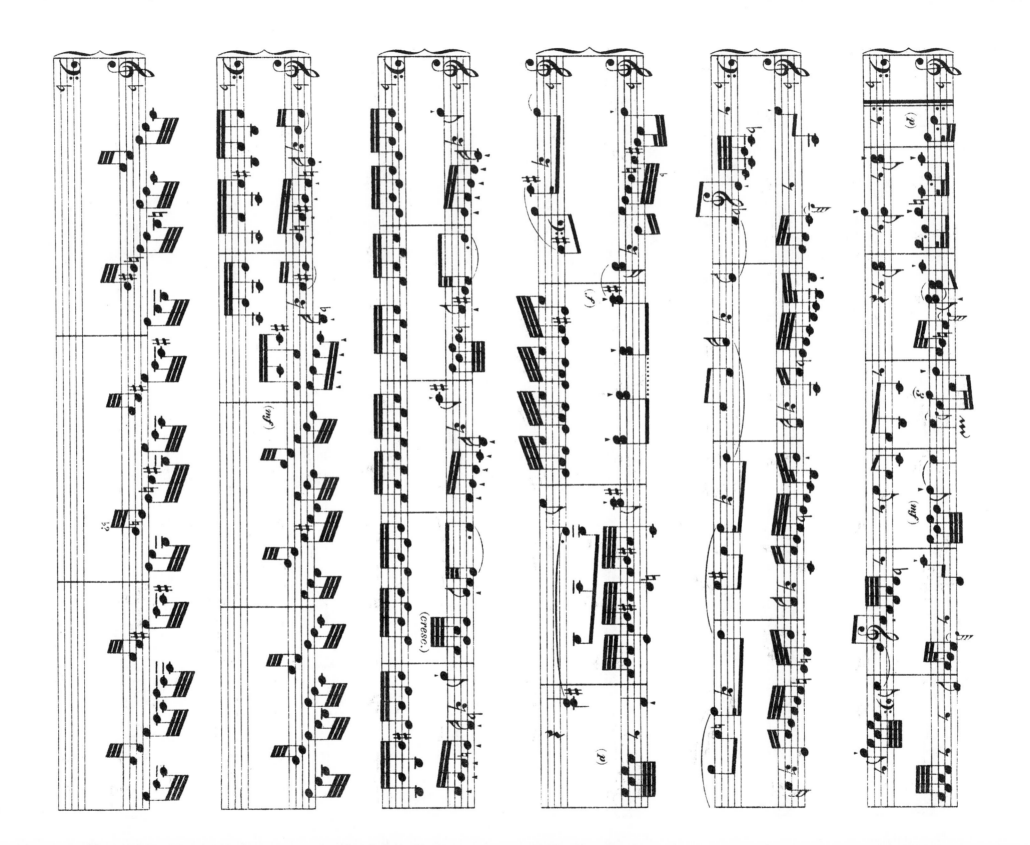

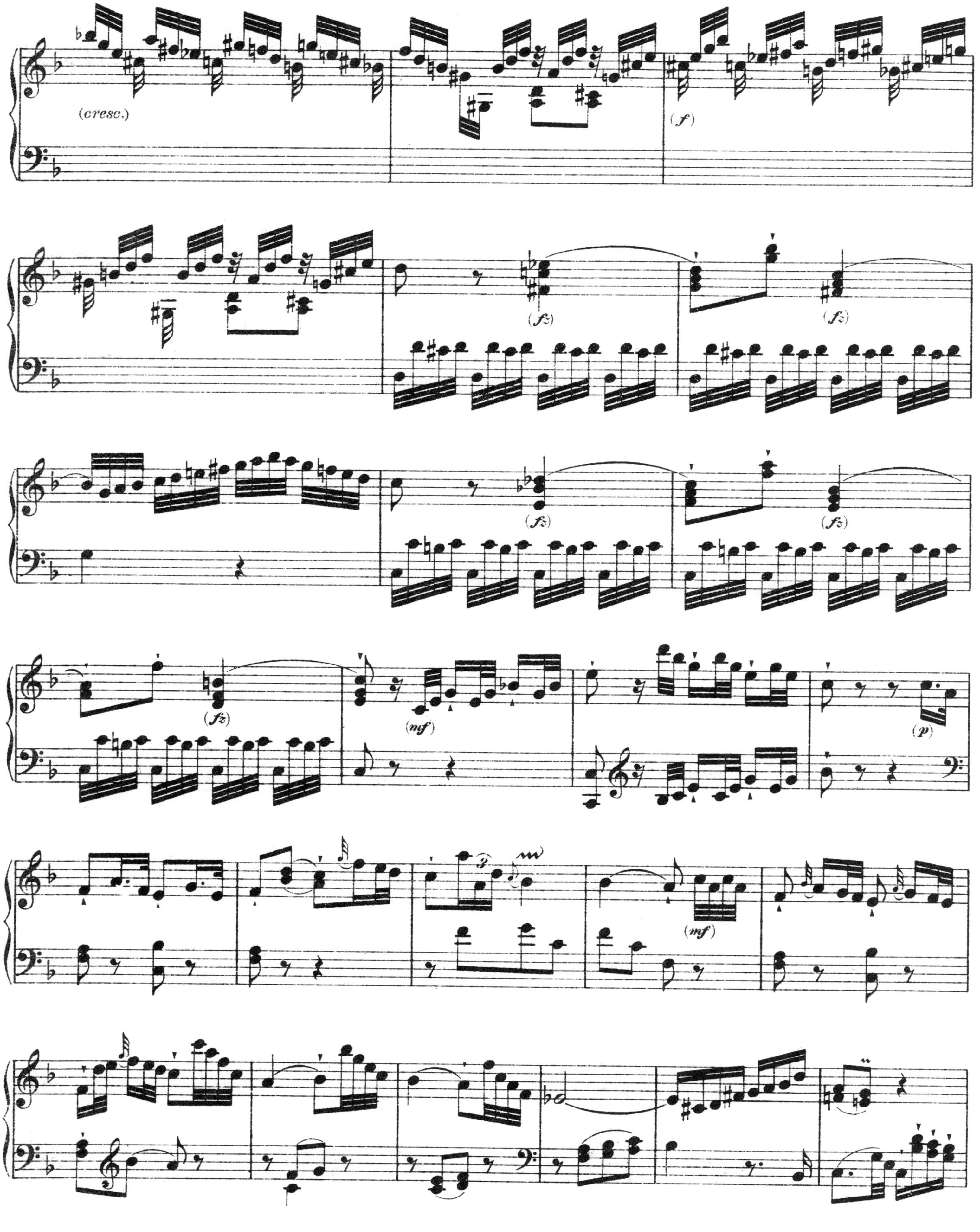
(cresc.)
(f)
(fz)
(fz)
(fz)
(fz)
(fz)
(mf)
(p)
(mf)

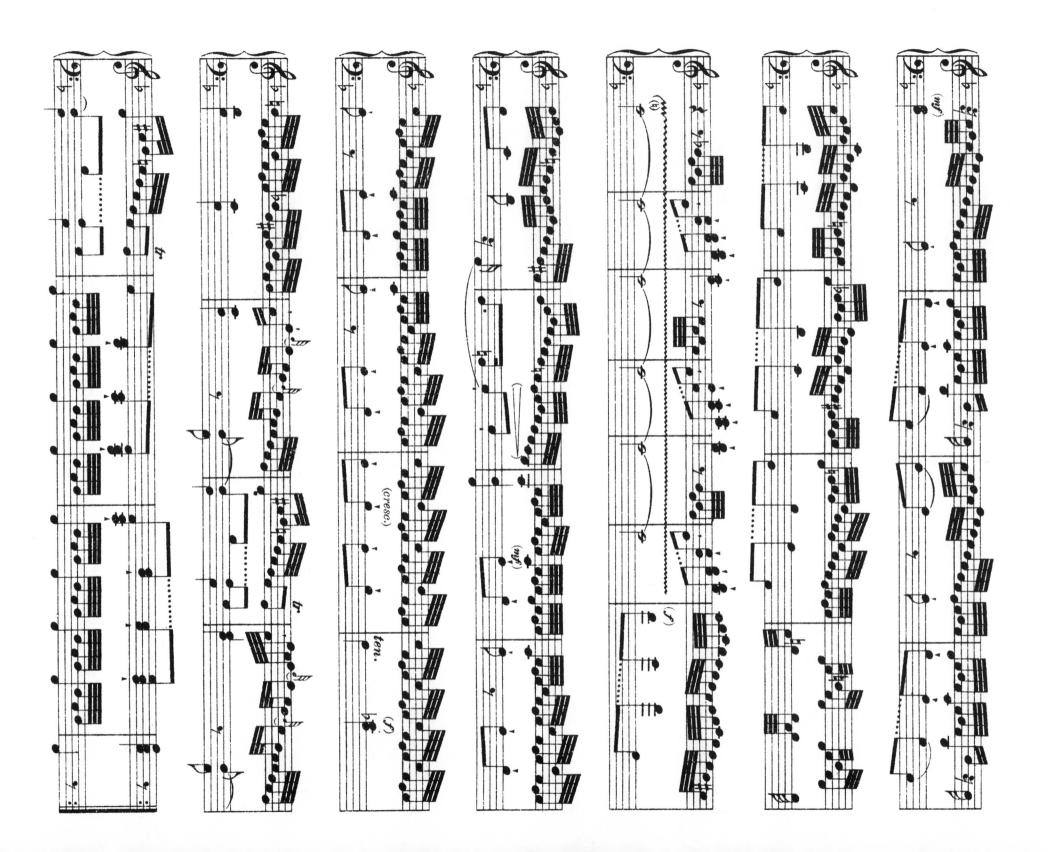

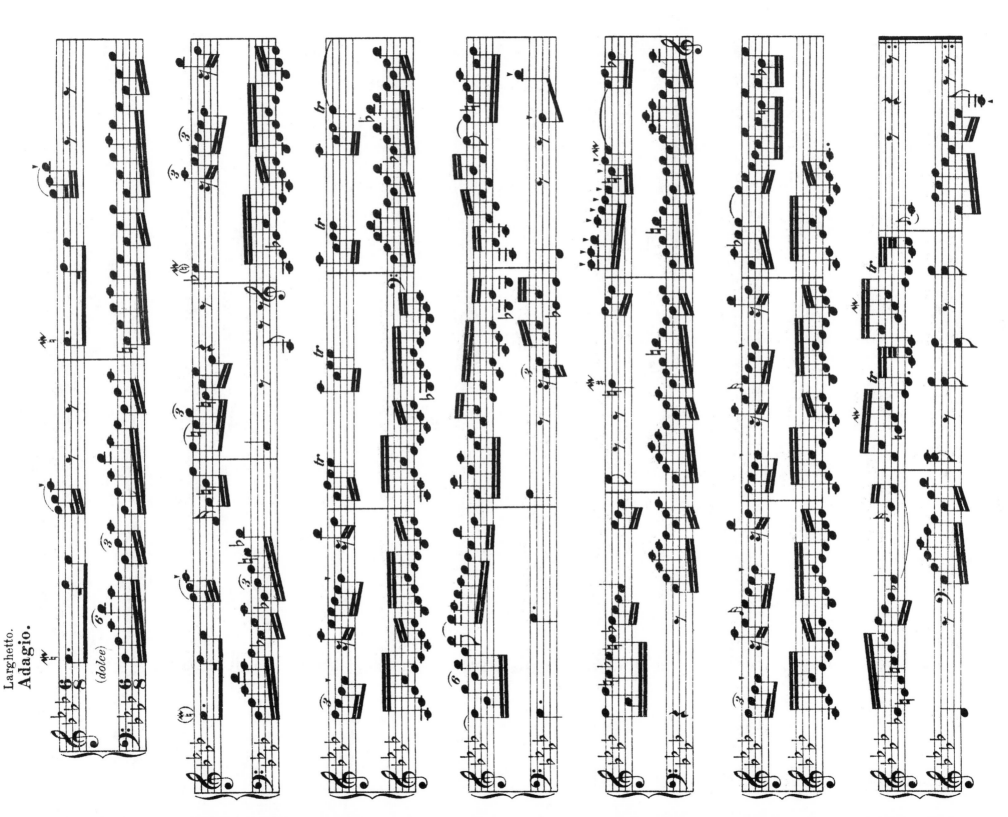

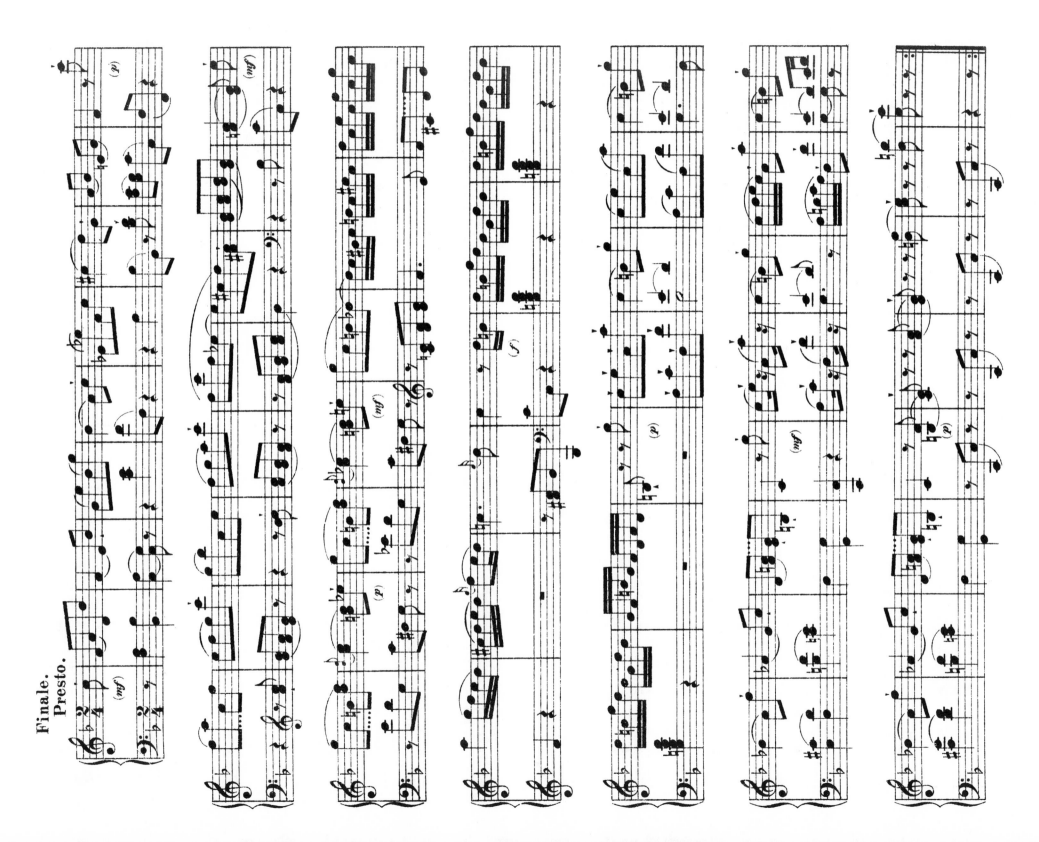

Finale.
Presto.

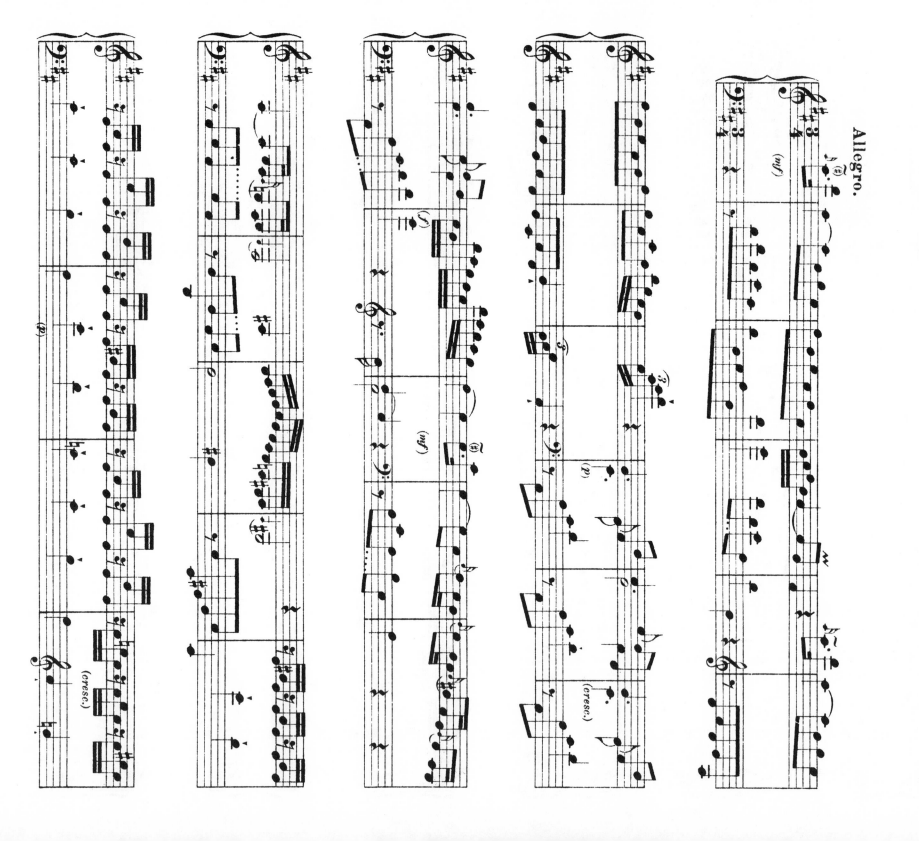

Sonata No. 24 in D Major

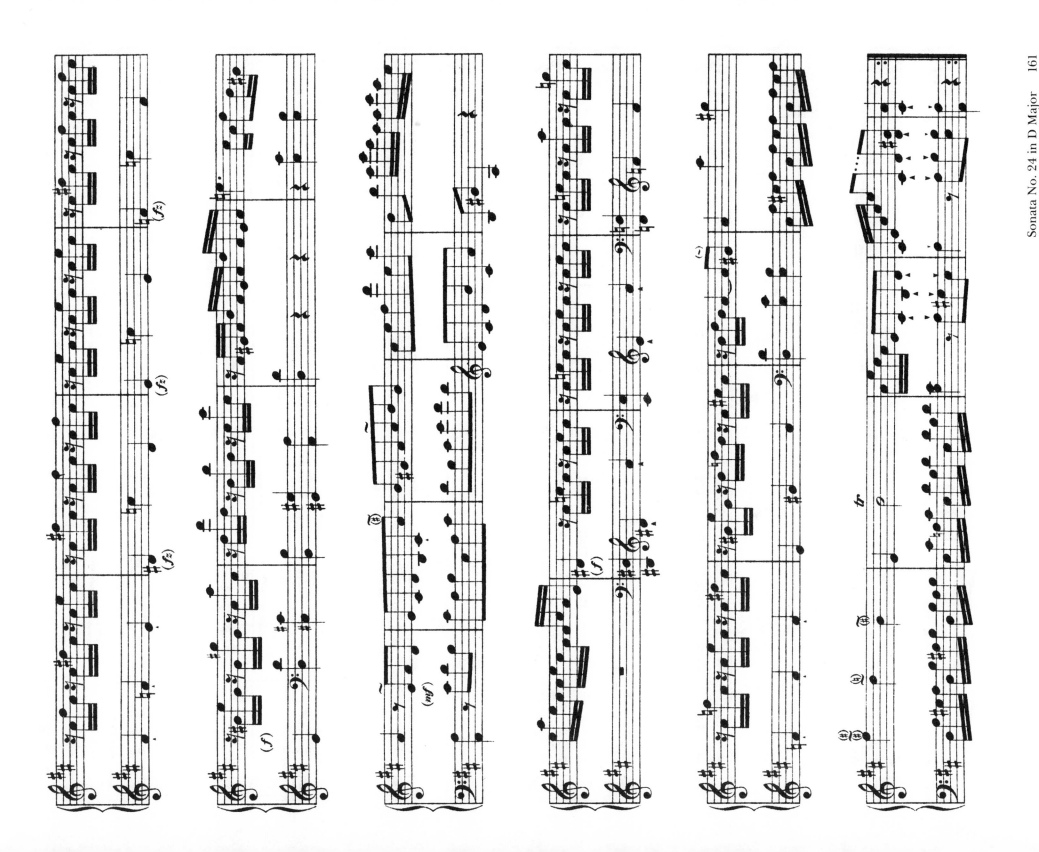

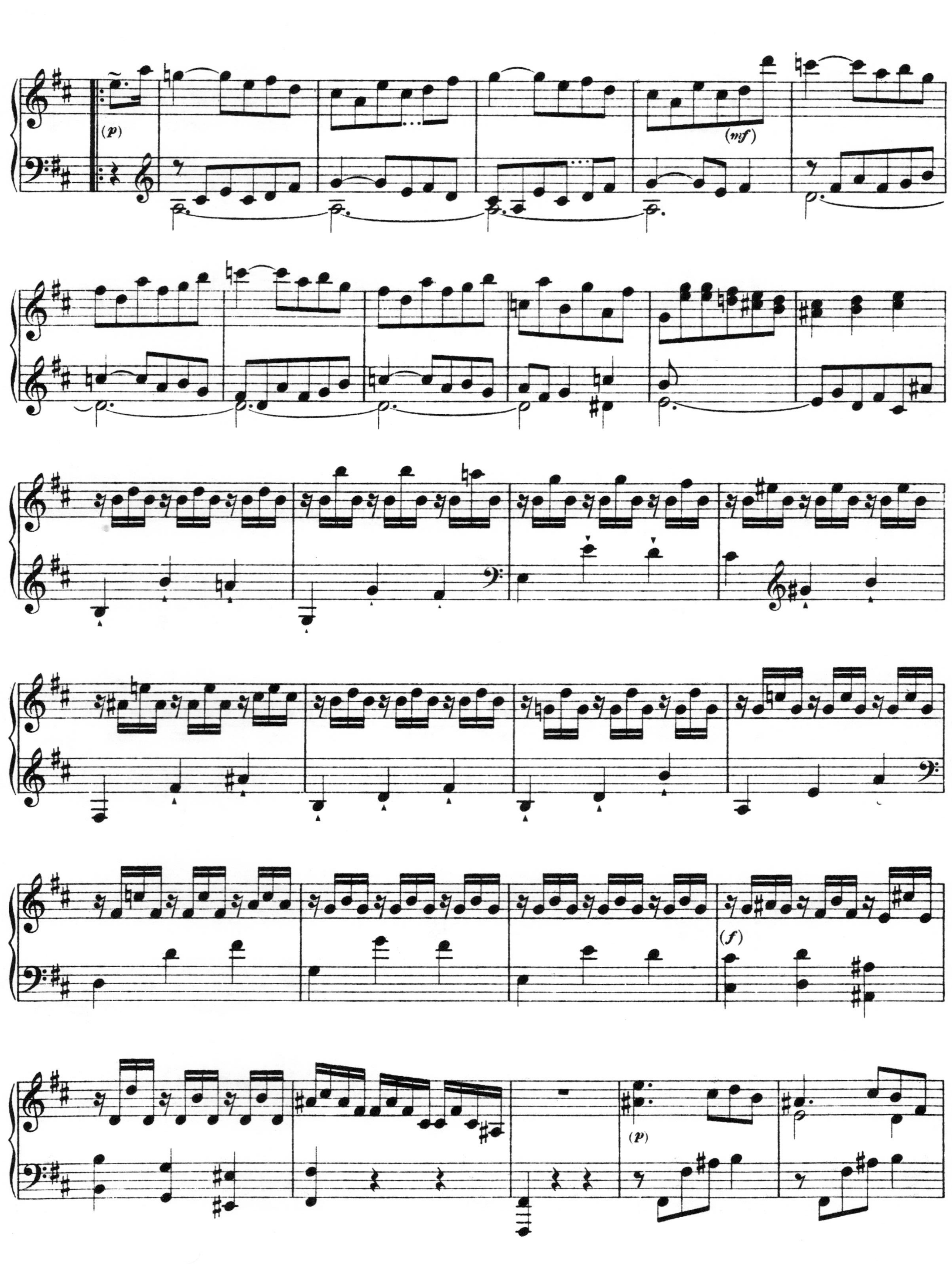
(p)
(mf)
(f)
(p)

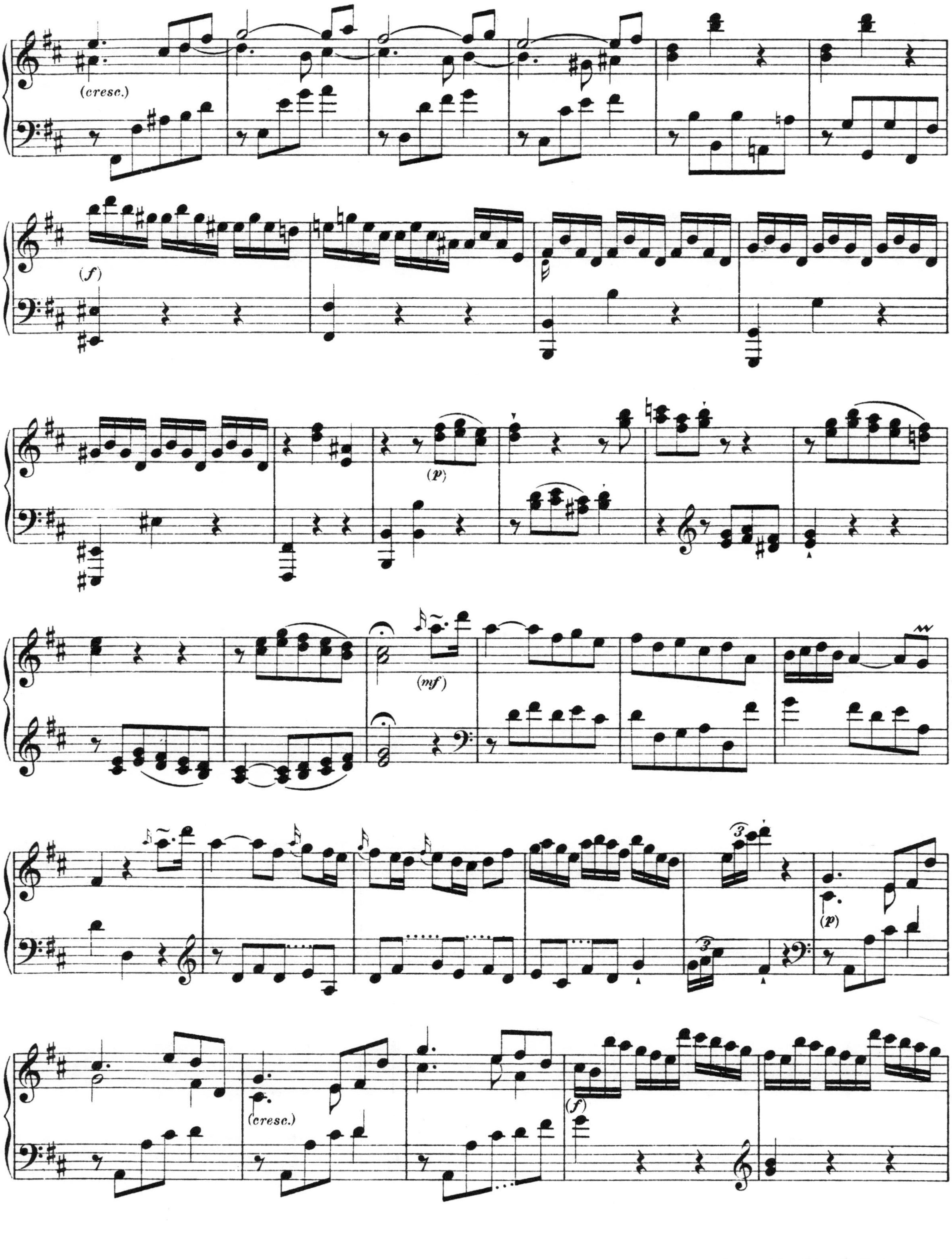
(cresc.)
(f)
(p)
(mf)
(p)
(cresc.)
(f)

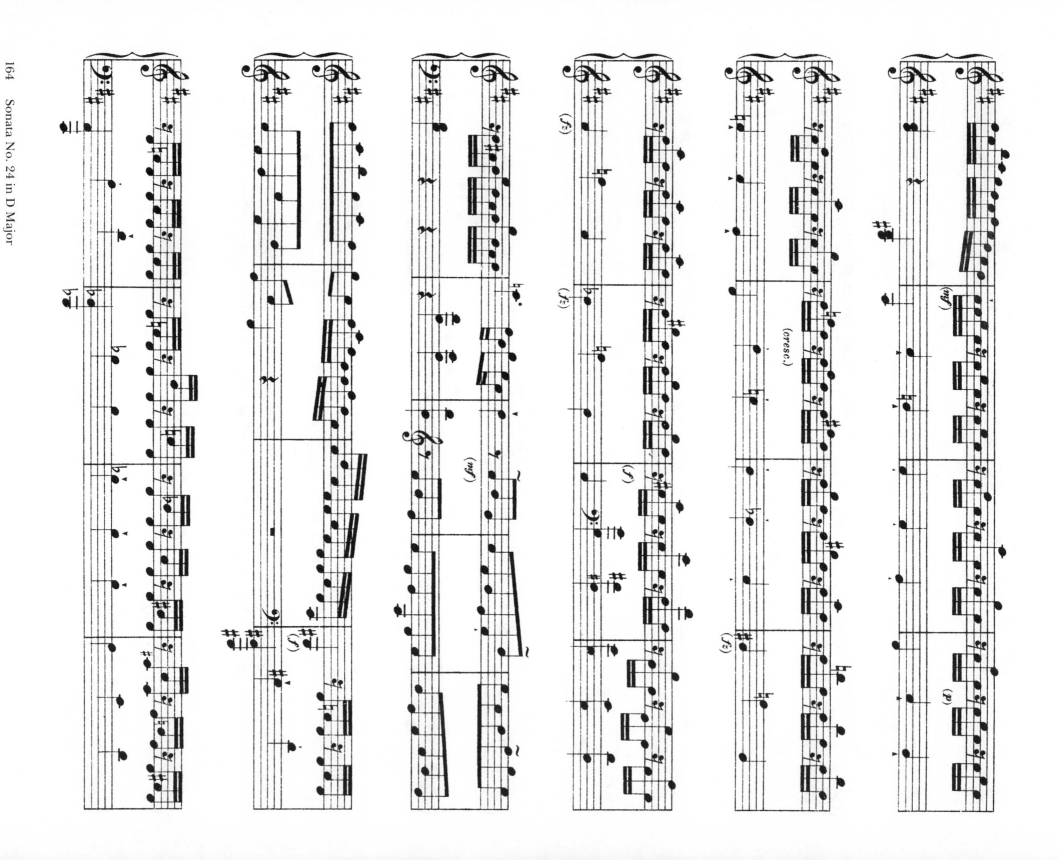

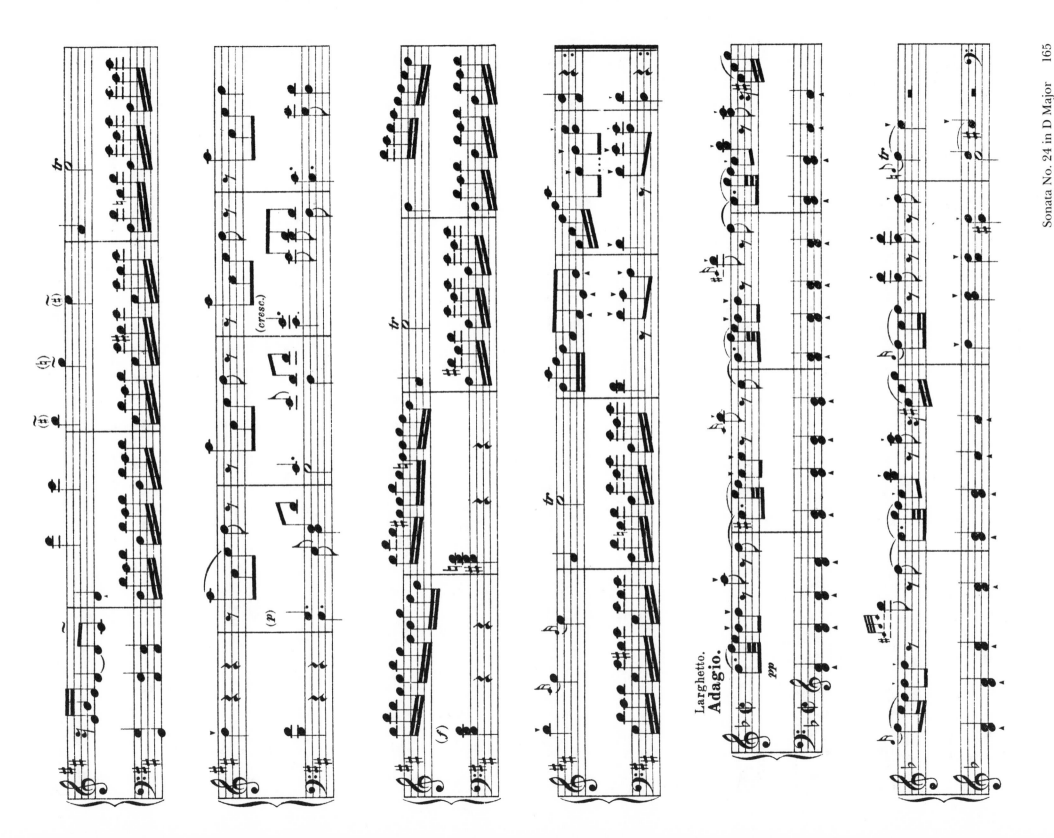

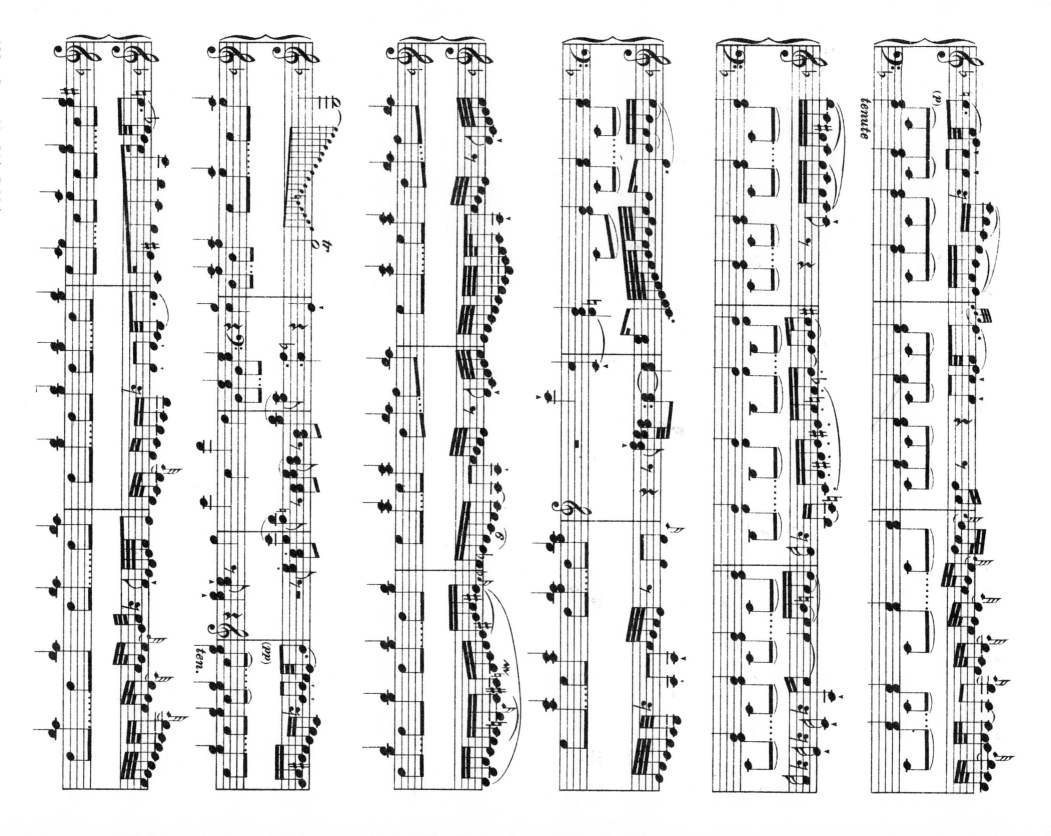

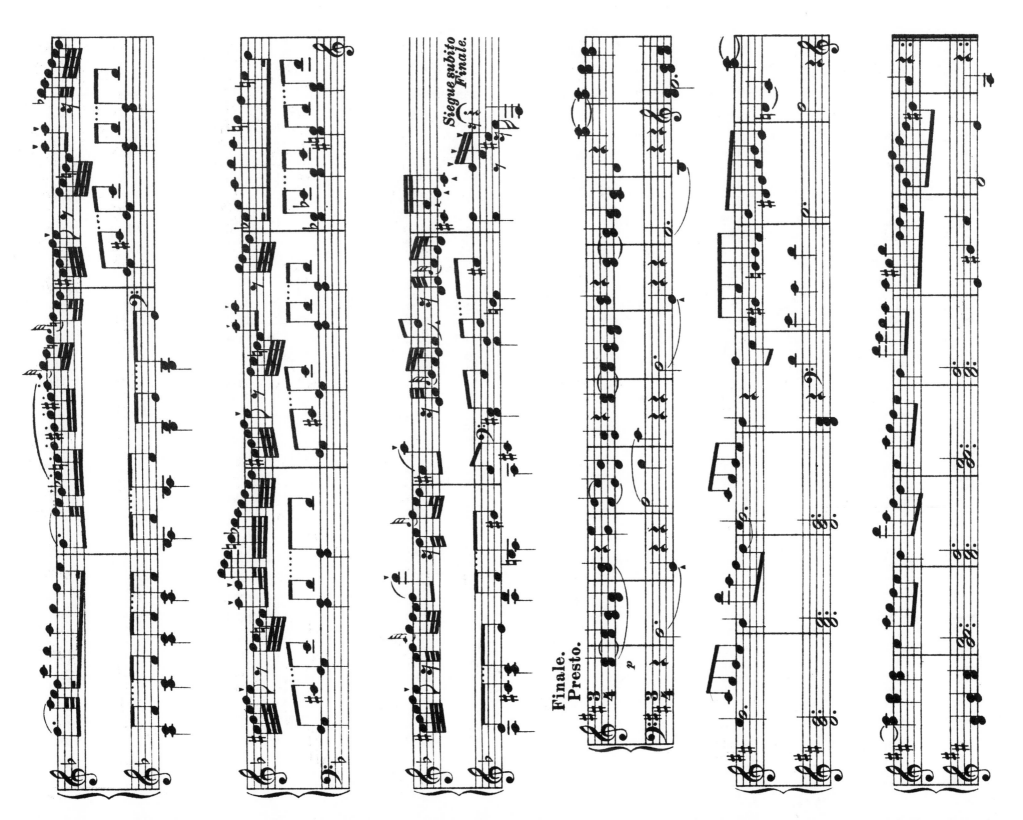

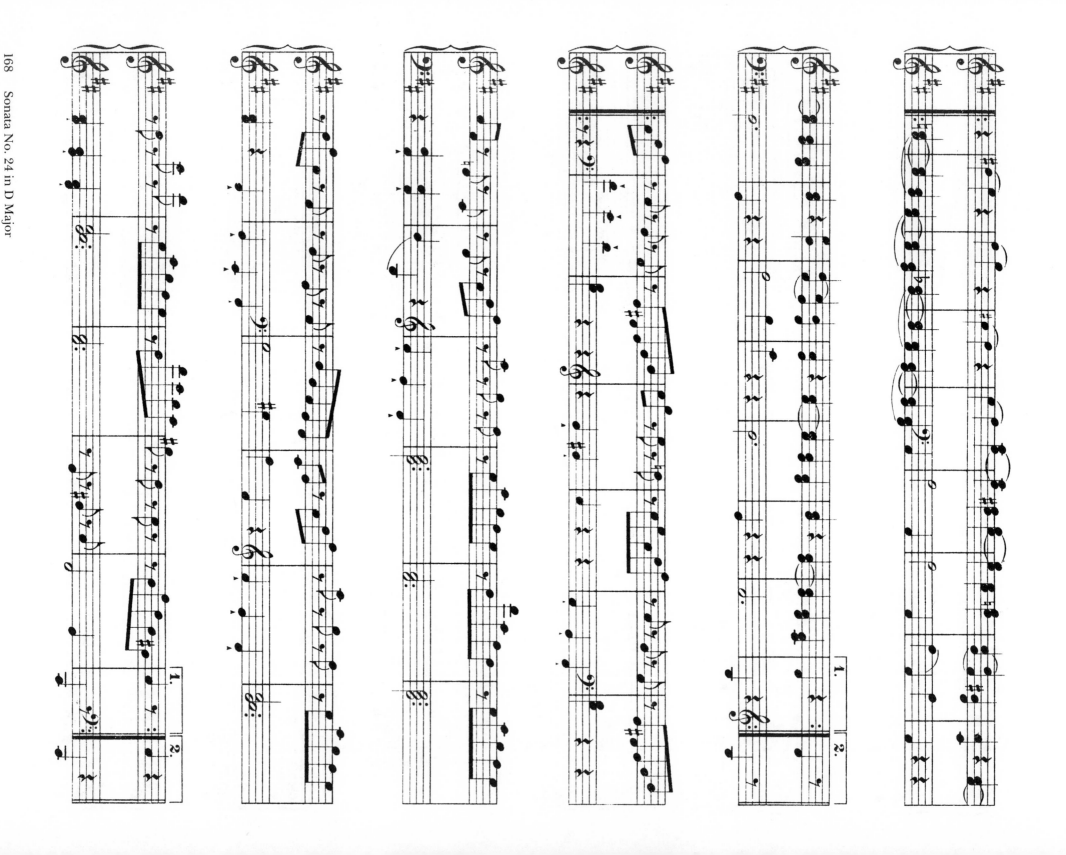

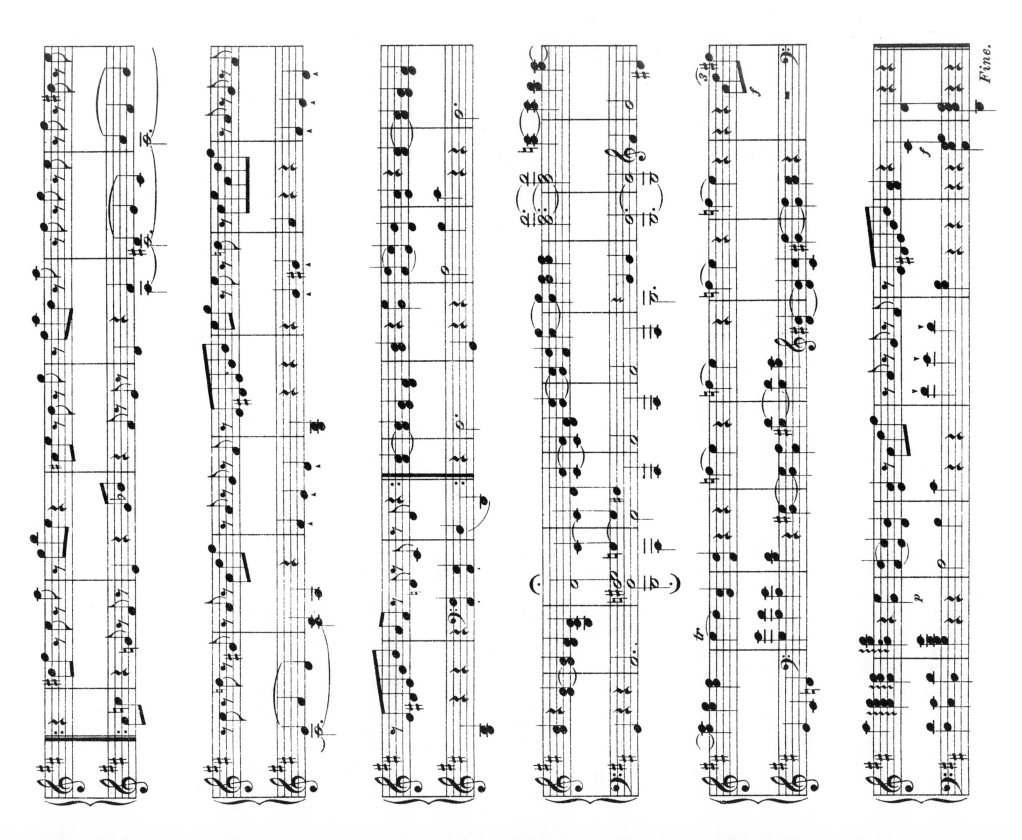

Fine.

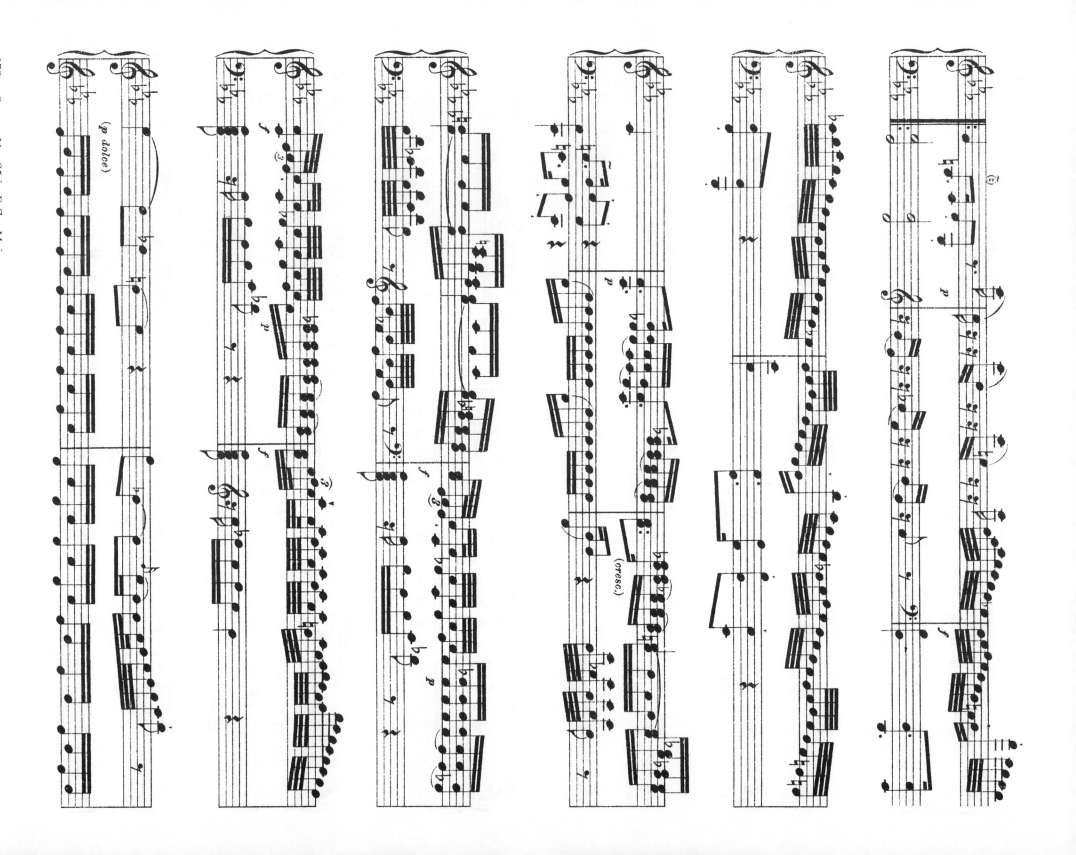

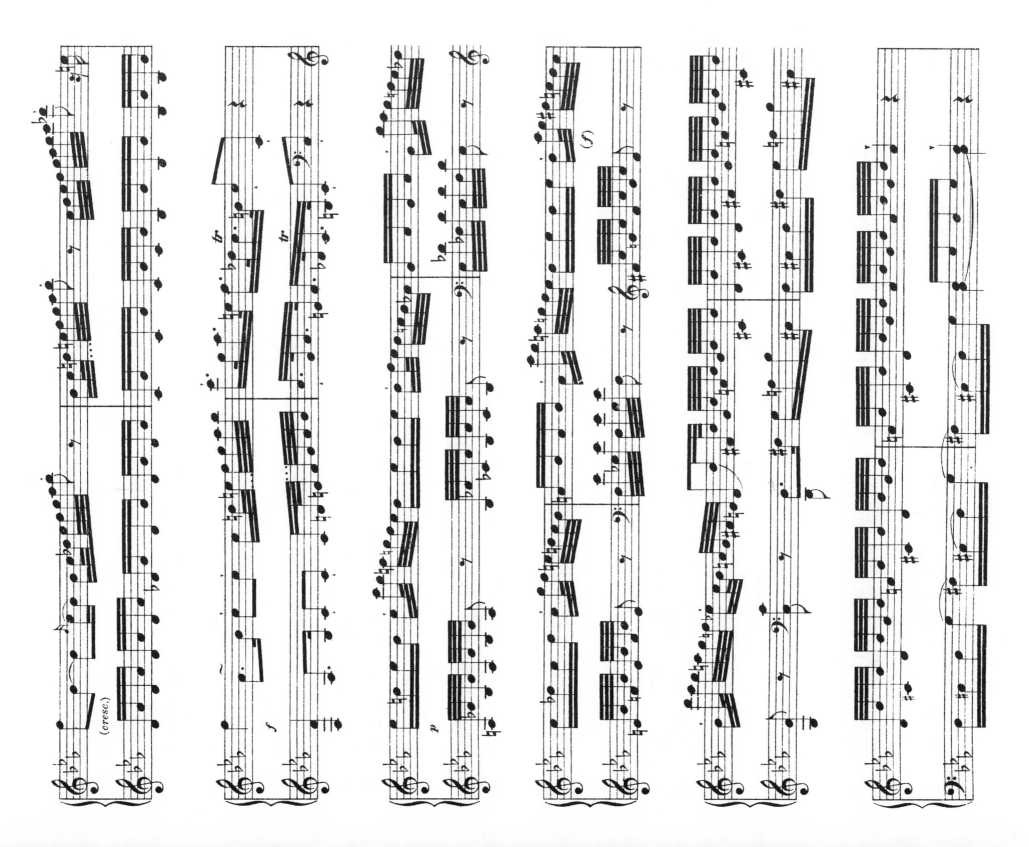

Tempo di Menuetto.

Imitazione

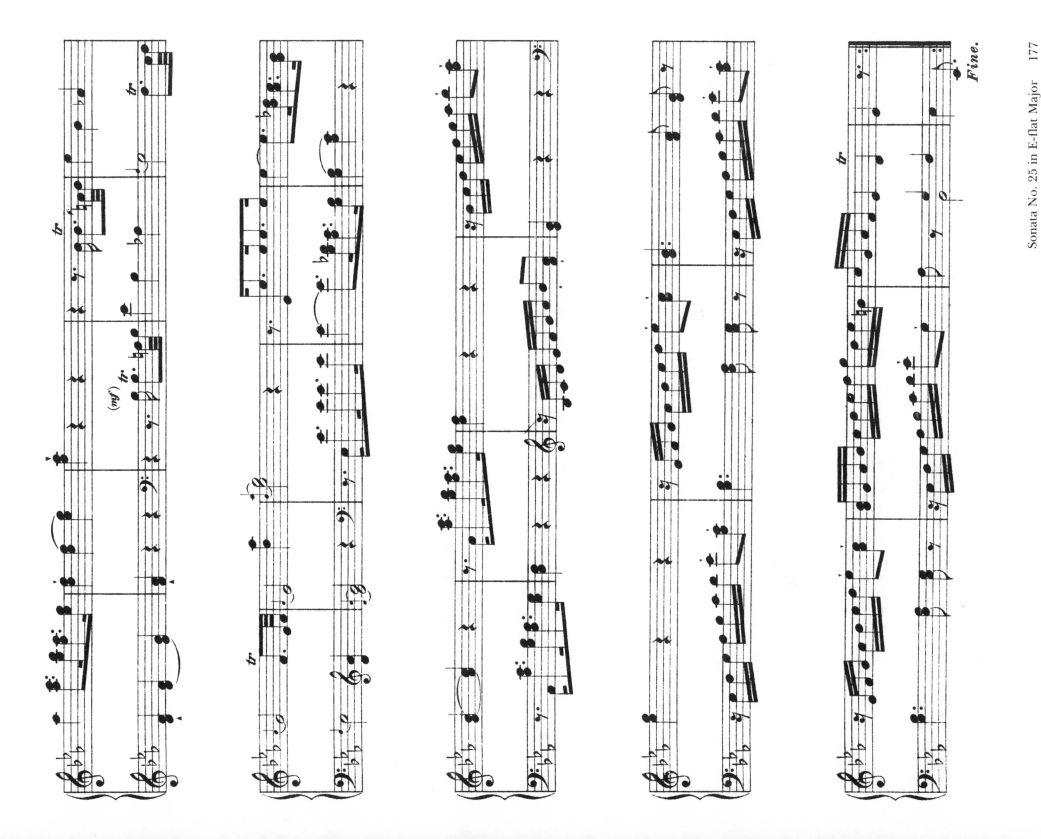

Sonata No. 26 in A Major

Allegro moderato.

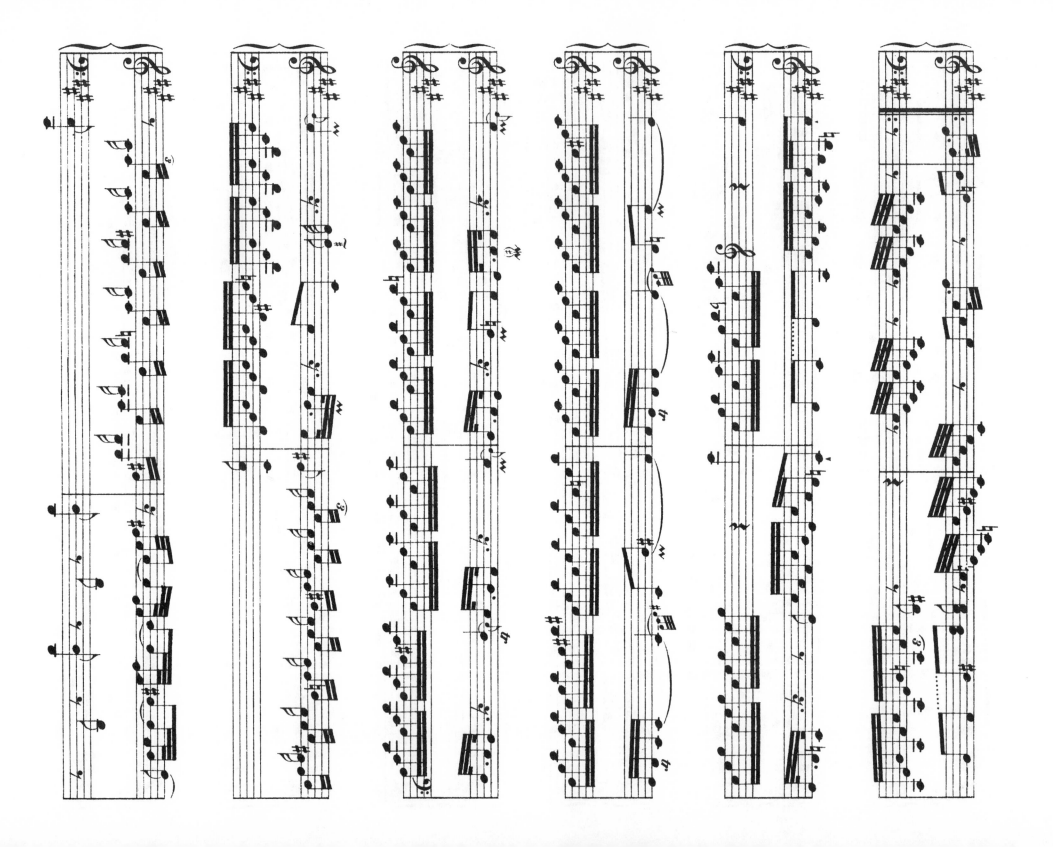

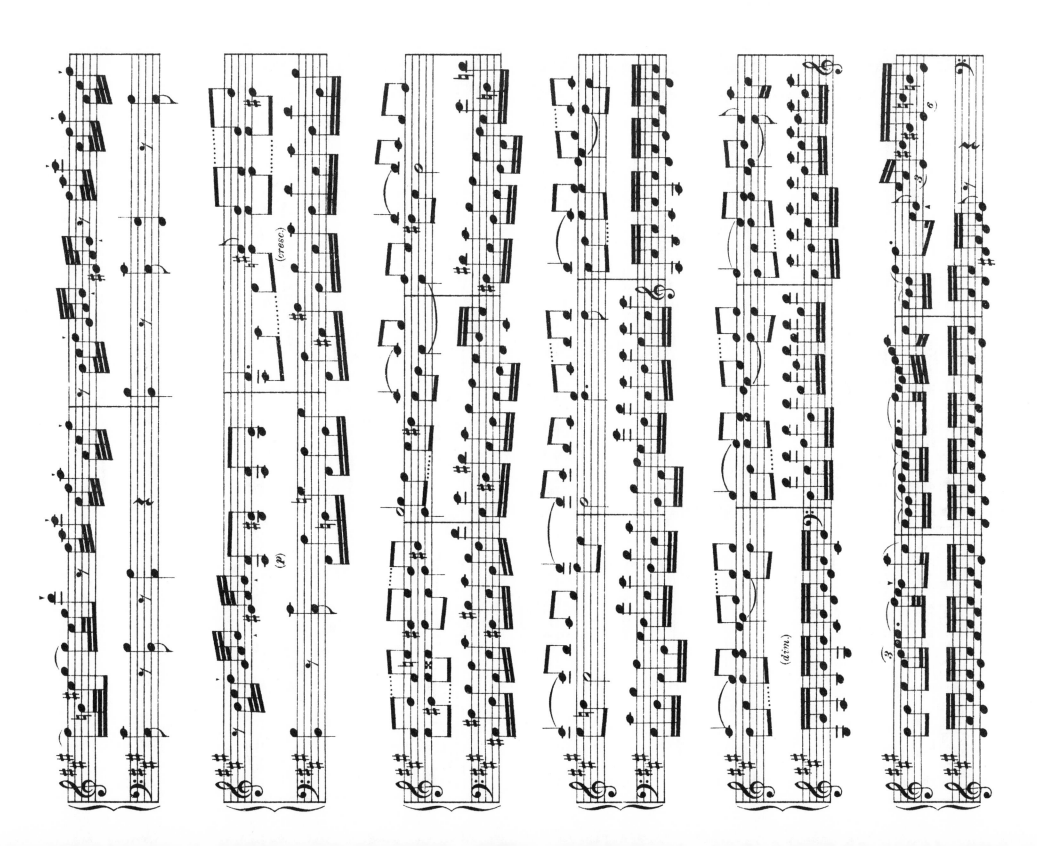

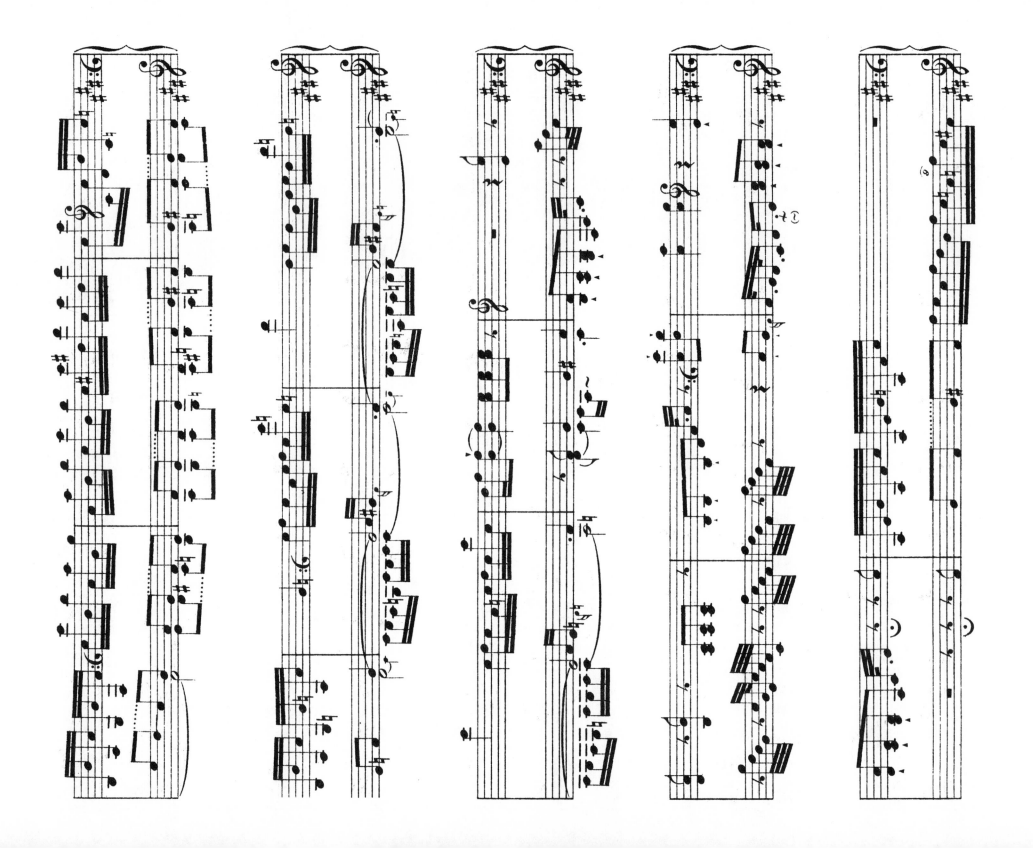

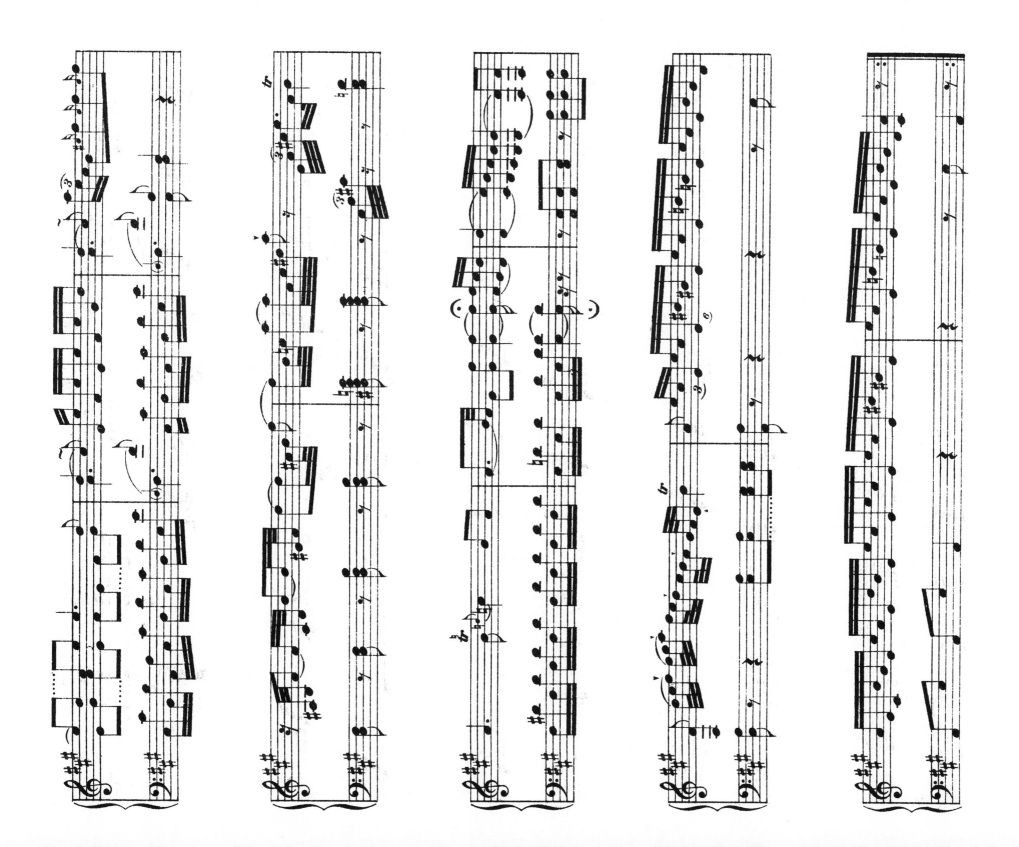

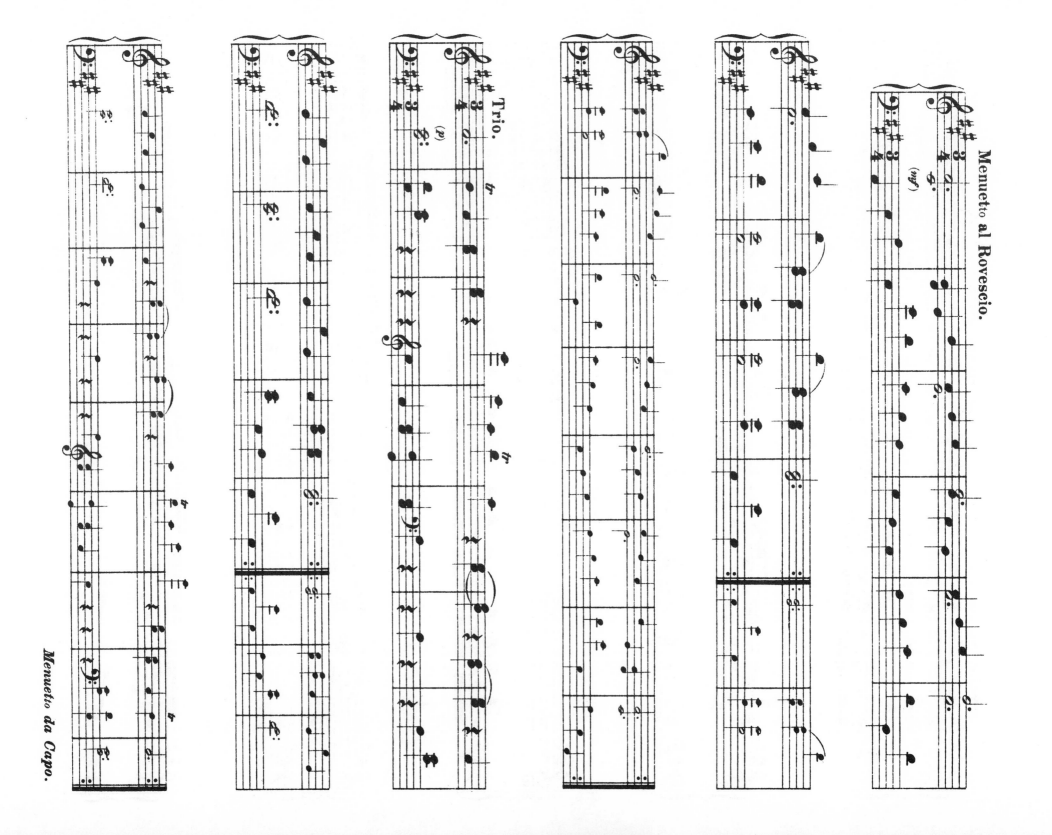

Sonata No. 27 in G Major

Allegro con brio.

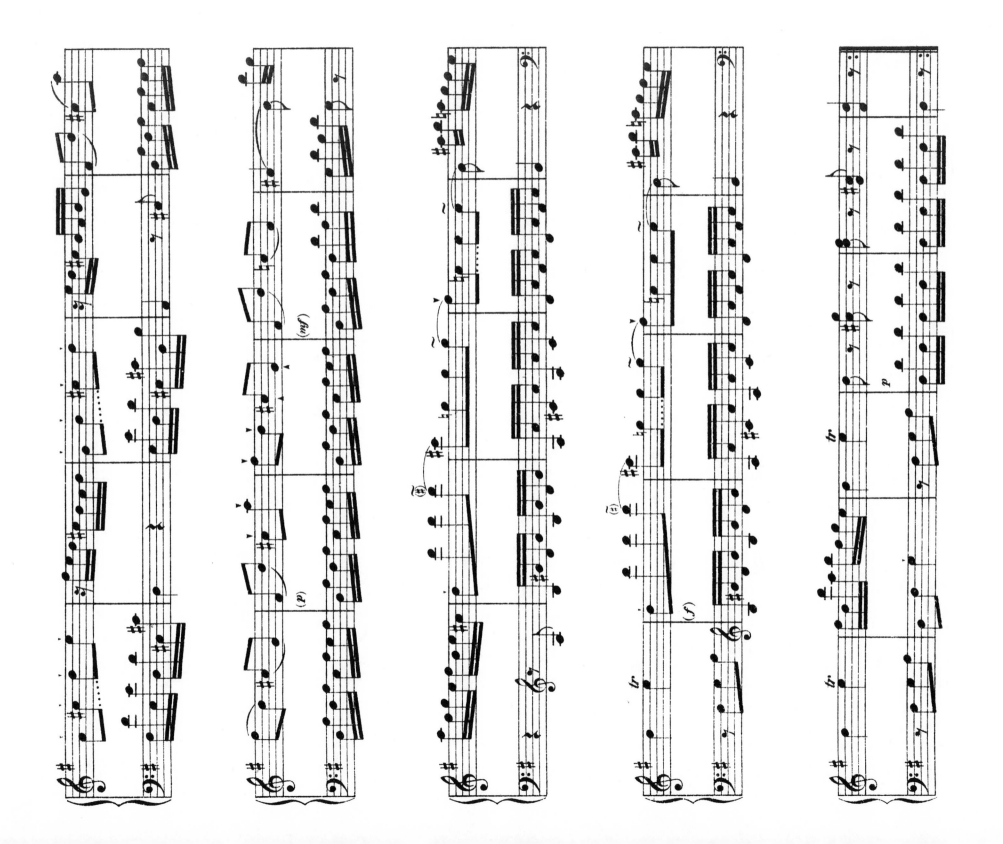

Menuetto.

Sonata No. 27 in G Major

Finale.
Presto.

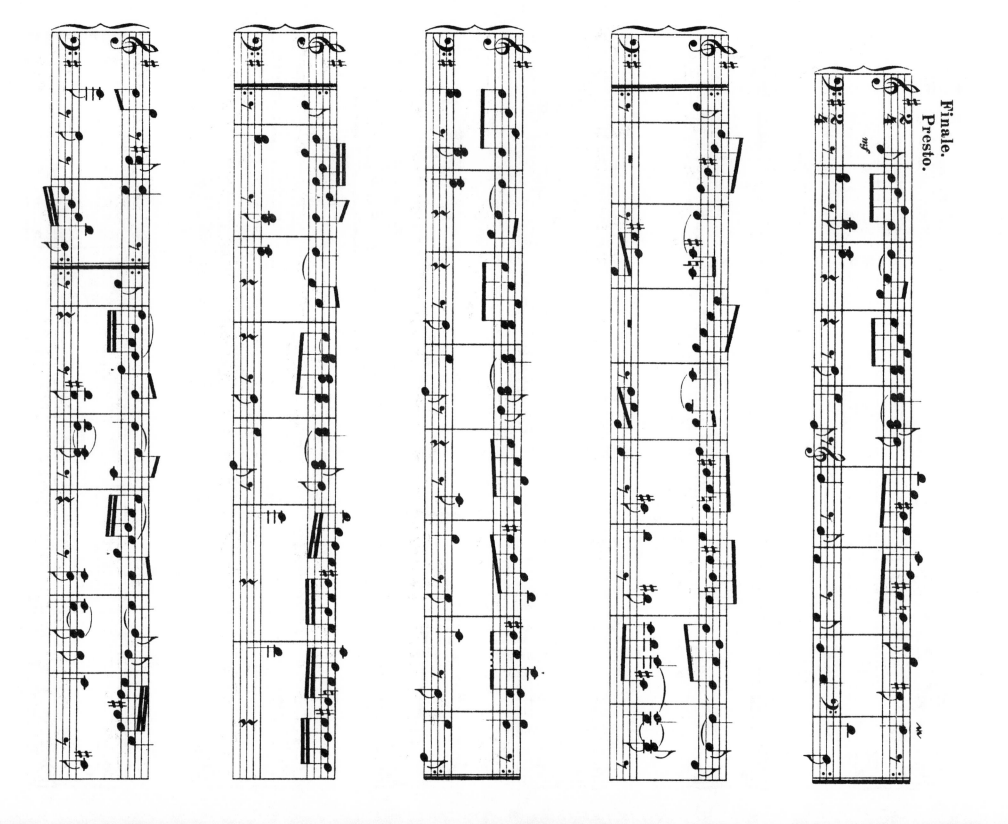

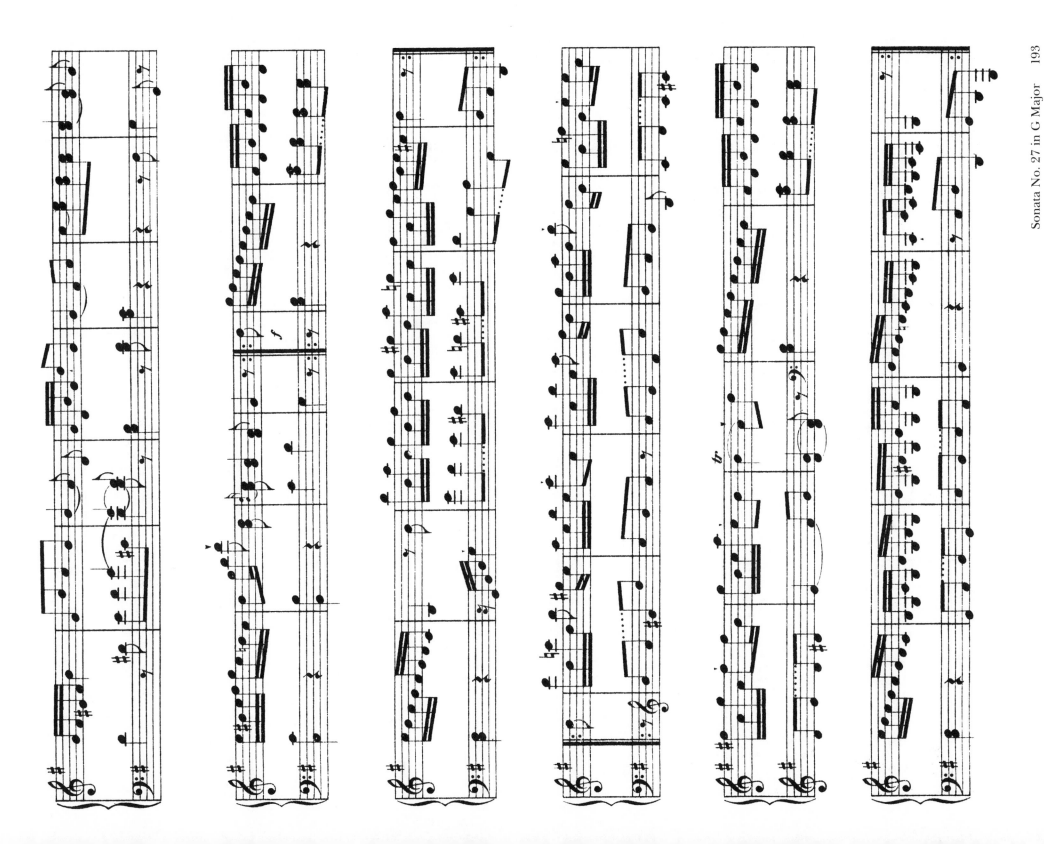

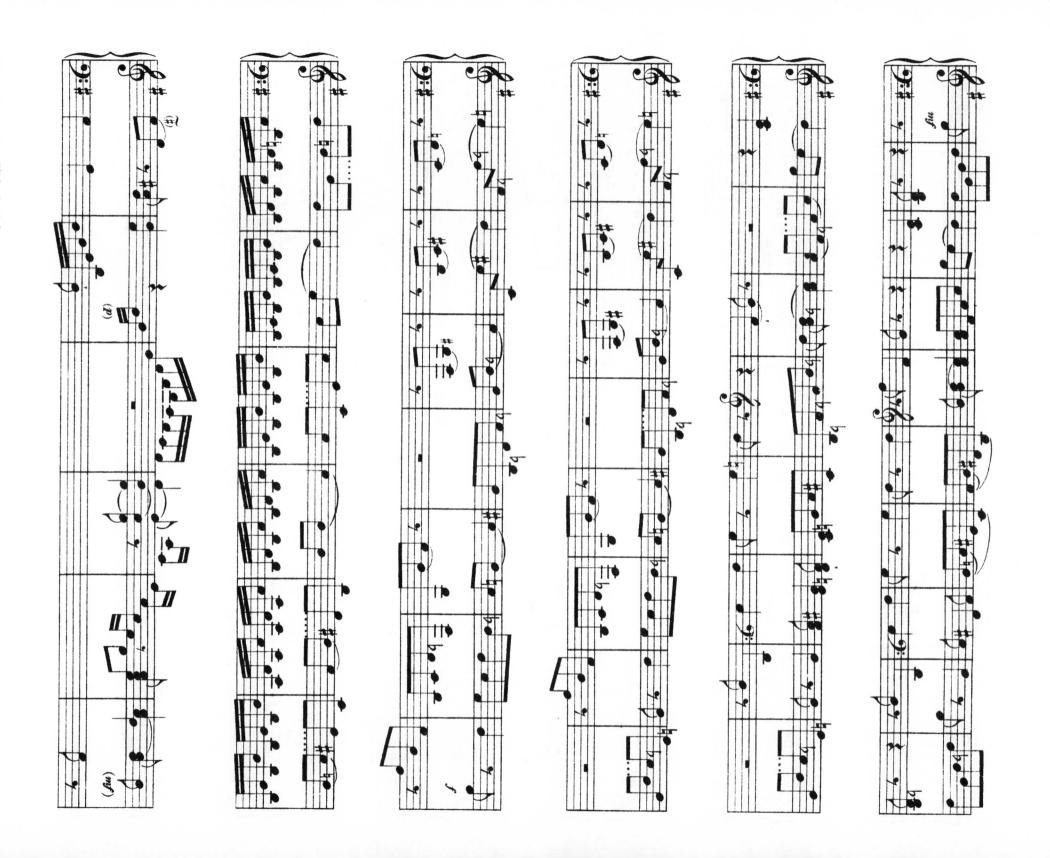

Sonata No. 28 in E-flat Major

Allegro moderato.

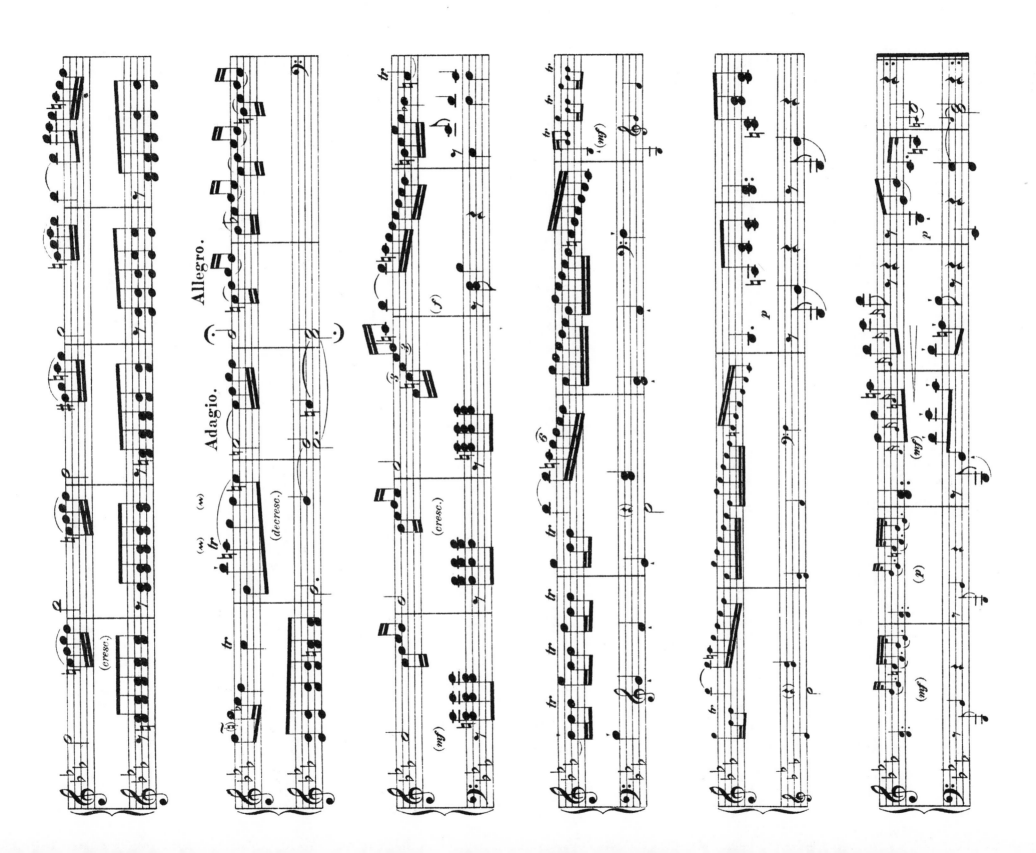

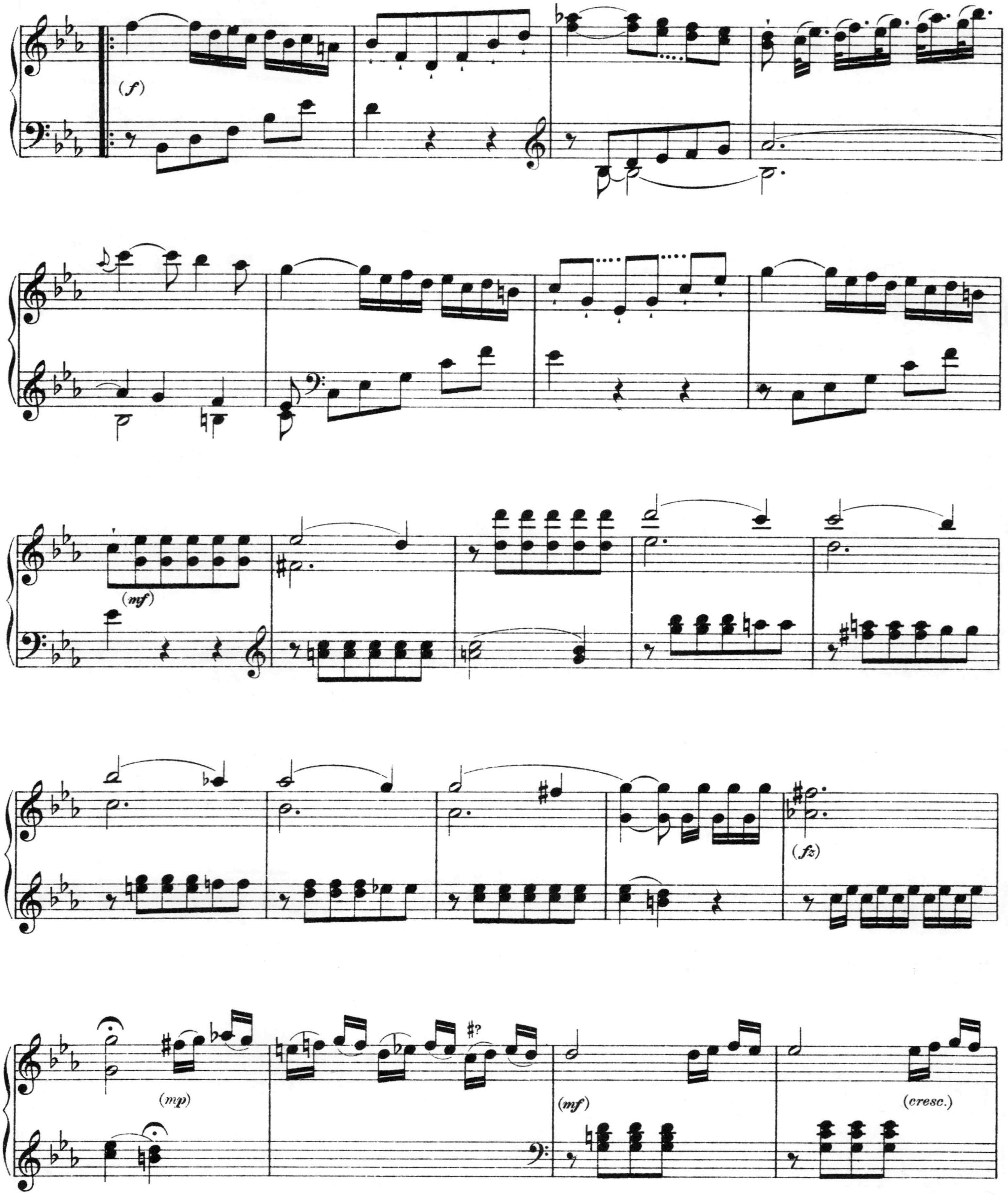
(f)
(mf)
(fz)
(mp)
(mf)
(cresc.)

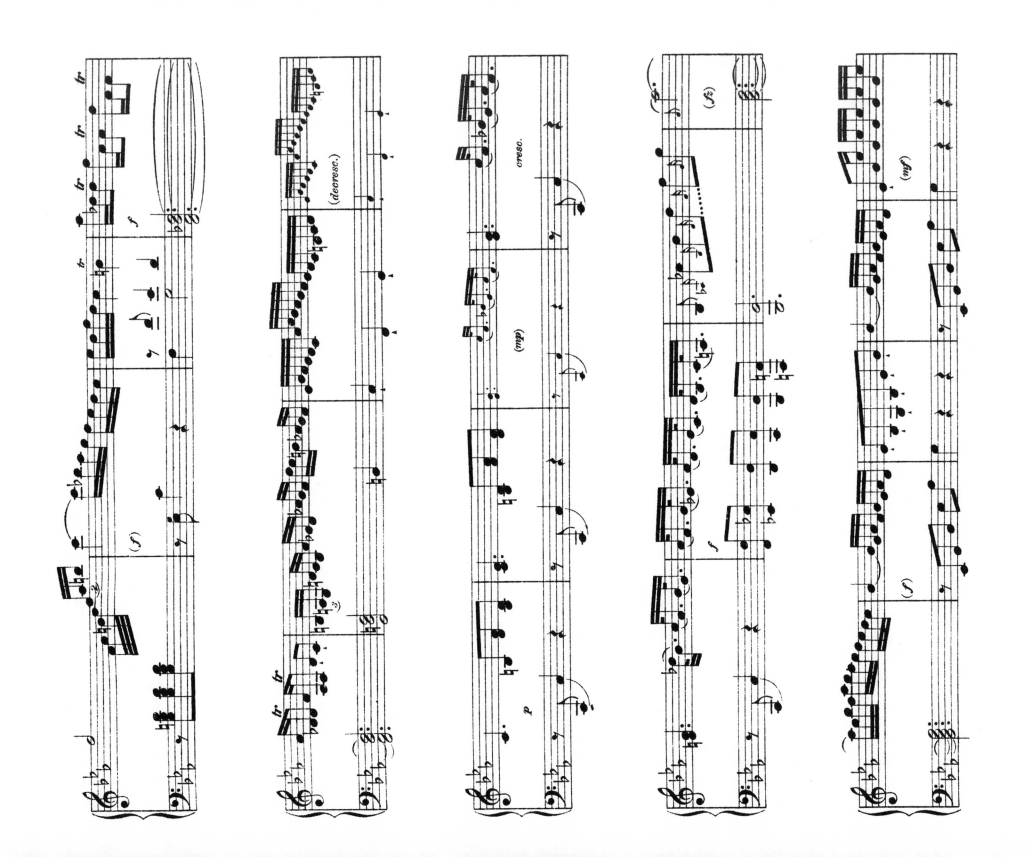

Menuetto.

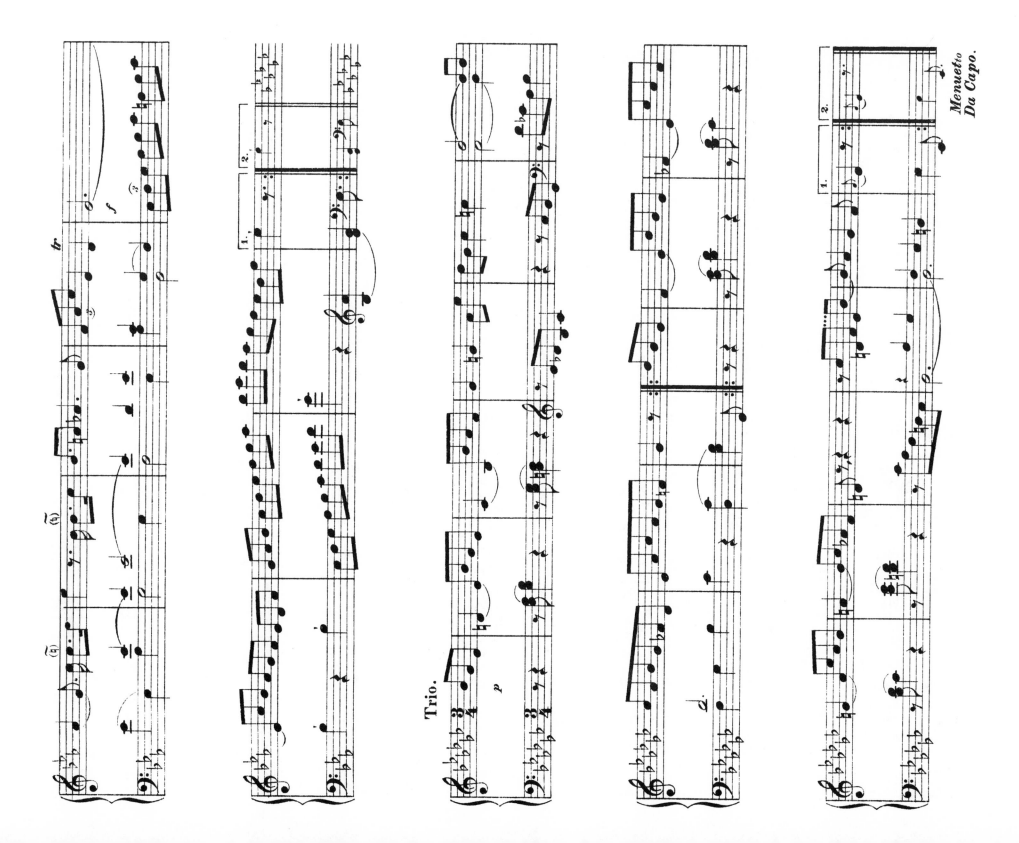

Finale.
Presto.

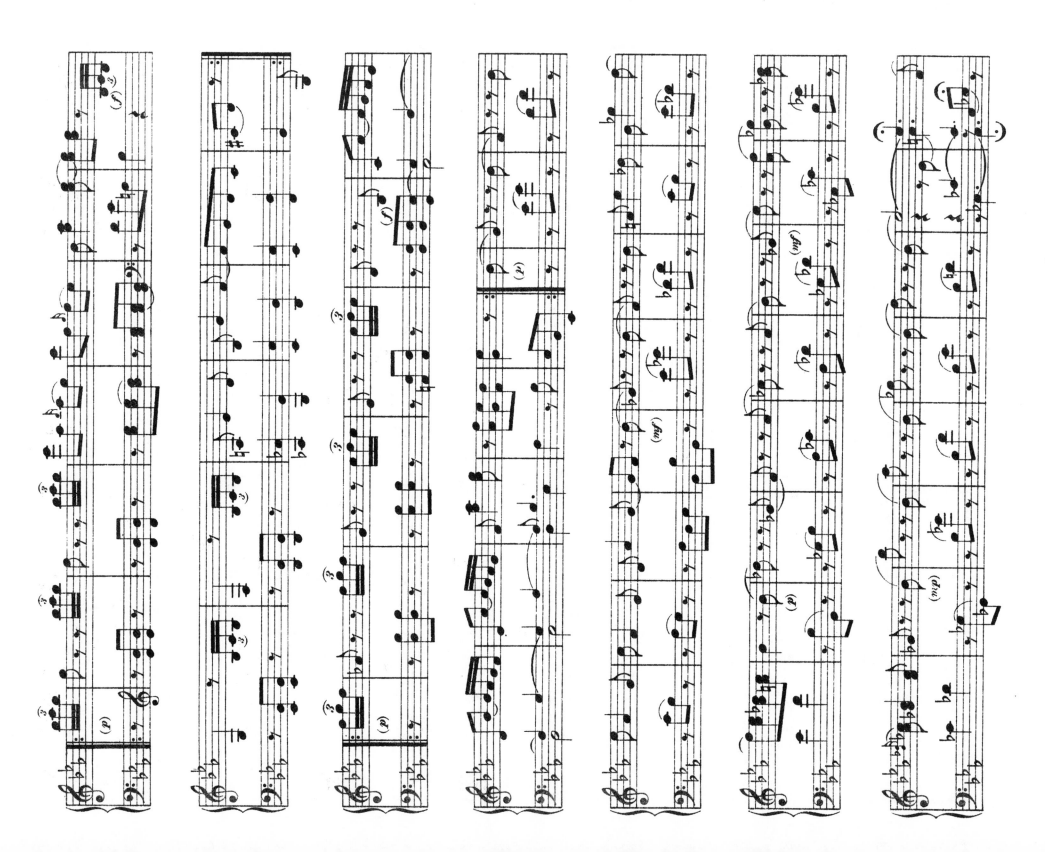

Sonata No. 29 in F Major

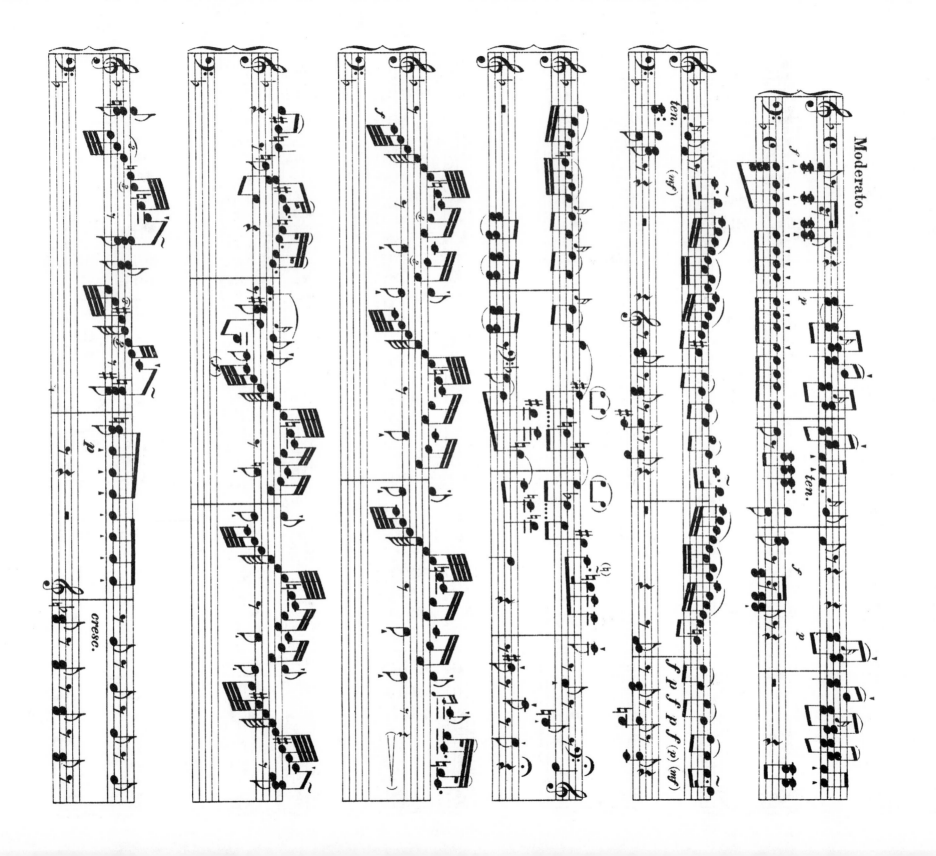

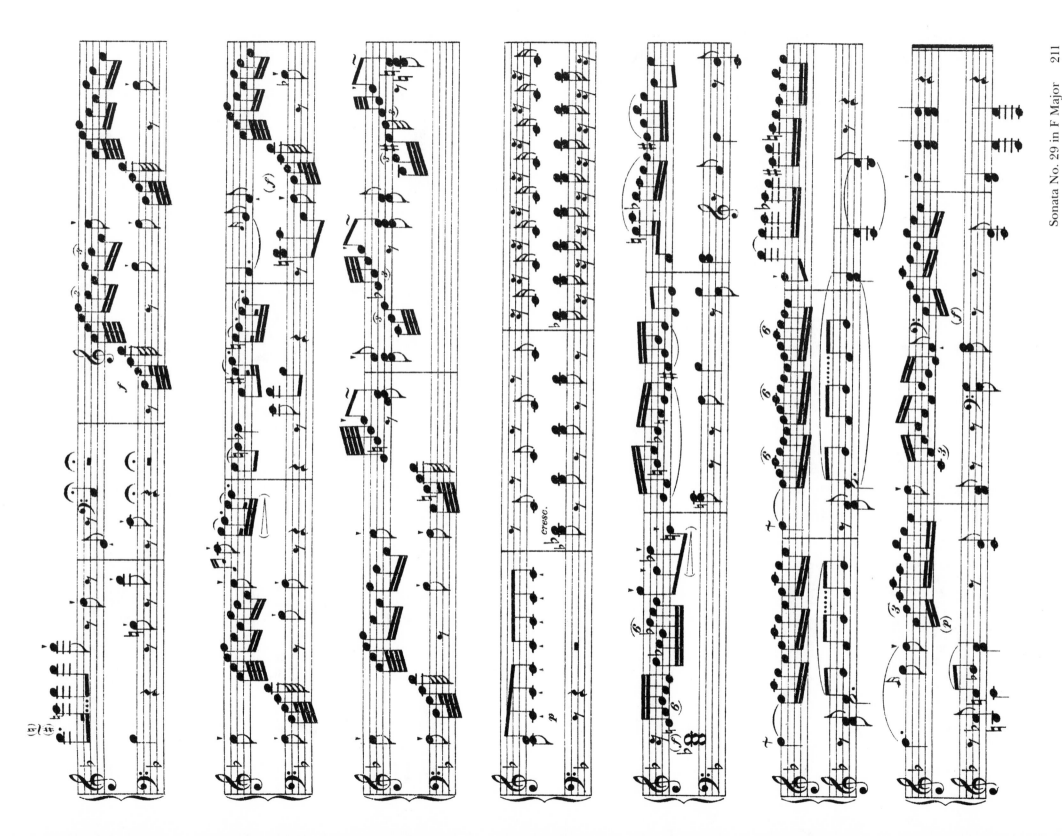

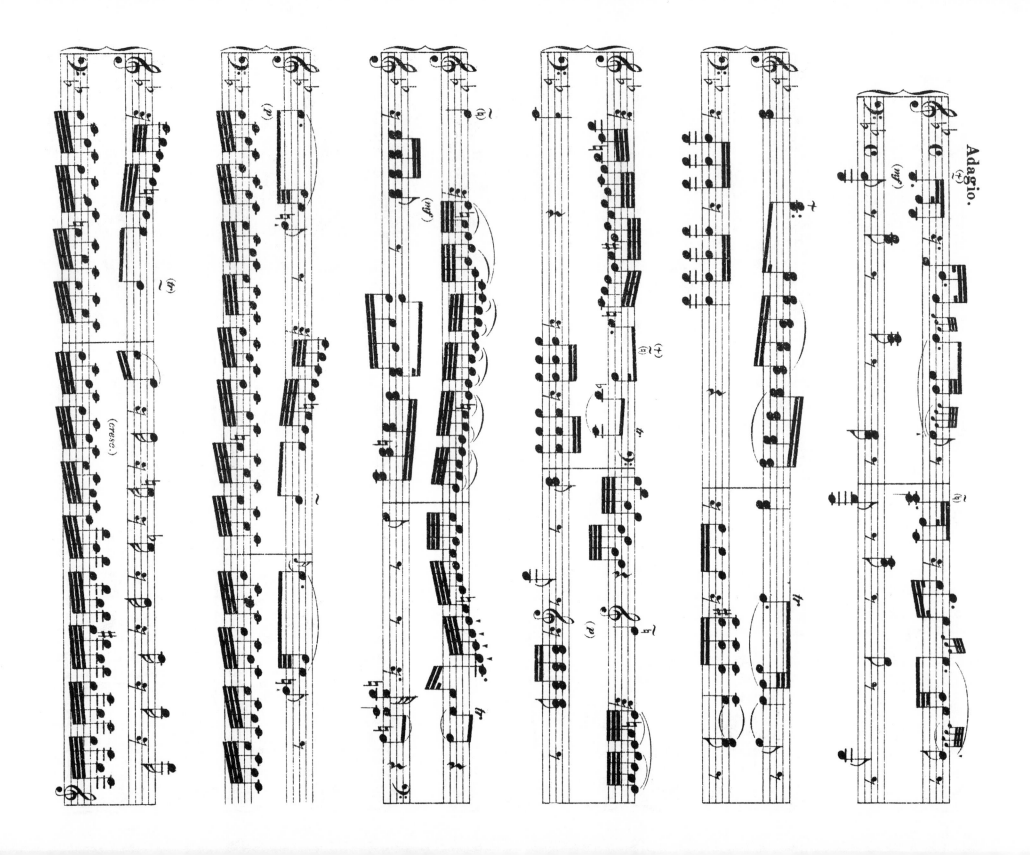

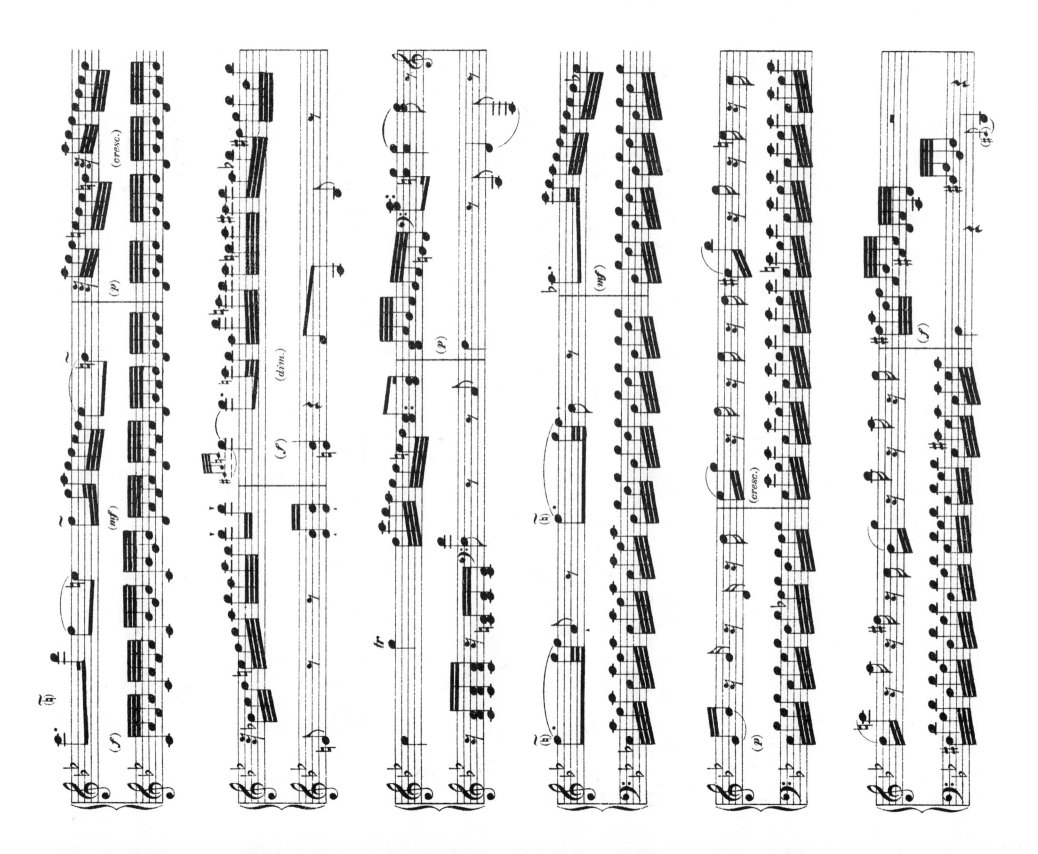

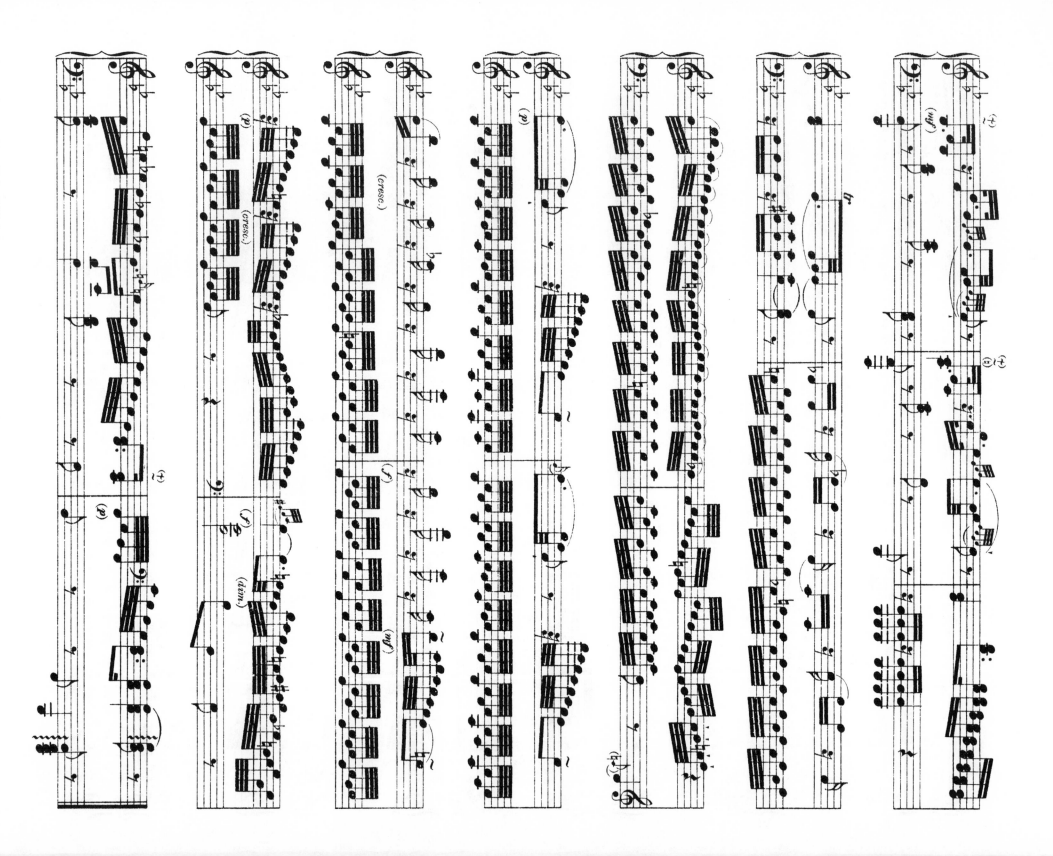

Maggiore.